Revisit, Reflect, Retell

UPDATED EDITION

Time-Tested Strategies for
Teaching Reading Comprehension

LINDA HOYT

HEINEMANN ✳ PORTSMOUTH, NH

Heinemann
361 Hanover Street
Portsmouth, NH 03801–3912
www.heinemann.com

Offices and agents throughout the world

Library of Congress Cataloging-in-Publication Data
Hoyt, Linda.
   Revisit, reflect, retell : time-tested strategies for teaching reading comprehension / Linda Hoyt. — Updated ed.
      p. cm.
   Includes bibliographical references and index.
   ISBN-13: 978-0-325-02579-7
   ISBN-10: 0-325-02579-7
   1. Reading (Elementary).   2. Reading comprehension.   3. Reflection (Philosophy).
4. Children—Books and reading.   5. Education, Elementary—Activity programs.
I. Title.
   LB1573.H69 2008
   372.47—dc22

                                                                          2008038208

Editor: Maura Sullivan
Production editor: Abigail M. Heim
Typesetter: Gina Poirier Design
Cover and interior design: Jenny Jensen Greenleaf Graphic Design & Illustration
Cover photography: Patrick Burke Photography & Graphic Design
Video producer: Bill Miller Film & Video Productions, Inc.
Manufacturing: Steve Bernier

Printed in the United States of America on acid-free paper

13   14   15   ML   4   5

To Maura
Thank you for your wonderful book titles,
creative thinking, and friendship.
Here's to bunny slippers, treasured pets, and
finding creative ways to connect the dots.

To Abby
Thank you for your patience, grace,
and unerring attention to detail.
You have the gift of making complex tasks
appear to be simple.
Thank you.

Dear Readers,

The quest for new knowledge and quality research to support effective practices in literacy education is unending... and that is good. As an educator with nearly forty years of experience and a commitment to advancing my own learning, it has been deeply gratifying to look back at *Revisit, Reflect, Retell* and discover that the instructional content is just as solid as it was ten years ago—*and new research backs it up!* New research not only makes the book more relevant than ever but also offers a wonderful opportunity to create fresh, new supports for students. This updated edition of *Revisit, Reflect, Retell* invites you to reacquaint yourself with time-tested favorites, and to explore additional possibilities through new tools for scaffolding multidimensional understanding.

In these pages you will find the influence of researchers such as P. David Pearson, Nell Duke, Richard Allington, Bob Marzano, and Michael Pressley, whose research has opened up so many important new insights. New tables have been included that organize lessons according to key comprehension strands to guide you as you plan units of study for comprehension (see pages xiii–xv). There are also direct links to Robert Marzano's Classifications of Thinking that will help you select the best experiences for processing text at a number of levels (see pages xvi–xix). In response to requests from readers, there are also wonderful new photos showing strategies in action across a wide range of grade levels, and a CD with full-color and customizable reproducible tools, plus a DVD with video footage showing me working with students.

I believe academic experiences should be like a tapestry, richly woven with opportunities for promoting reflective, critical thinking, and environments that resonate with high-quality talk. When students engage in reflections that range from clarifying and summarizing to drawing interpretations and synthesizing, they learn that comprehension is a deeply satisfying, active experience.

This book is filled with suggestions for ways to engage learners as thinkers, as communicators, and as readers who understand that the primary goal is to comprehend. But I offer a caution: The learning experiences in these pages are *not* time fillers. They are meaningful investigations that support communicative competence and understanding. Too many students encounter learning situations in which they do little more than get through an assignment and comply with teacher directions. They don't get excited about ideas; they aren't actively involved as readers. It is my hope that the learning opportunities offered in this book bring those very students into a state of attention and interest—a state where problem solving, critical thought, and peer dialogue resonate with purposeful wonder.

As you use this resource, I encourage you to approach the reproducibles as springboards for your own creativity. Enlarge the spaces for writing or expand thinking with invitations that challenge students to reach deeper and think in new ways. These are learning experiences that can be explored from your own perspective or linked to your own state standards. Best of all, these learning experiences can be explored on plain paper! Challenge yourself and your students to use these tools to help you build an environment that is alive with rich learning and spirited conversations about text.

While comprehension is a deeply personal exploration that is enhanced by strategy use, we must remember that comprehension instruction isn't about a single book or a single strategy. In designing comprehension instruction, it is vital that students develop a strong sense of how to reach for understanding, and how to be strategic as they navigate print. What they learn today should help them read more deeply in the *next* text they select. As you consider opportunities for active comprehension, please also consider the following:

1. Am I asking my students to engage in learning that is significant, learning that will shape them as lifelong learners who question, wonder, and challenge their own understandings?

2. Is this experience one that will help these learners reach for knowledge that is deep and multidimensional, rather than shallow and superficial?

3. Have I helped the students see how the learning could transfer to their interactions with other texts?

4. Does the task require social engagement and the use of academic language? Does the vocabulary of the learning "float on a sea of talk"?

5. Is this experience a necessary scaffold to understanding, or would these learners be better served simply by reading another selection?

Welcome to *Revisit, Reflect, Retell: Updated Edition*. A world of possibility awaits.

Sincerely,

Linda Hoyt

Linda Hoyt

FOREWORD

When I first read the first edition of Linda Hoyt's popular book, *Revisit, Reflect, Retell: Strategies for Improving Reading Comprehension*, I was amazed and surprised. "Who is this woman," I asked myself, "and how did she manage to get the comprehension revolution just right? How did she provide something so practical, yet so reflective of all we have learned about comprehension in the past thirty years?" And now, with this updated and expanded edition, she gets it even "righter"—if that is possible. At any rate, she has once again brought a remarkably useful resource to her teaching colleagues.

What makes Linda's book so useful is its simultaneous grounding in solid theory and research about reading comprehension and in the everyday world of classroom practice. In the final analysis, it is Linda's uncanny ability to provide fellow teachers with down-to-earth, practical activities they can use in their classrooms that sets her book apart. In good conscience teachers can feel free to use any or all of the activities, including the reproducible graphic organizers, to promote and in some cases assess students' comprehension of a wide range of texts. All the while teachers can be comfortable in the knowledge that what they are providing is just what their students need to make progress in the all-important process of improving their comprehension.

Two aspects of her approach demand special notation. First is the skilled manner in which she employs graphic organizers. These are important tools for all students, but they are doubly important for that subset of students who must "see" the relationship of ideas in pictures or spatial relationships rather than in words. Visual displays of information are visual representations, or, as I like to say, visual re-presentations; they literally re-present the same information to the students and, in the process, make it more accessible and more memorable. Second is her dedication to active student learning through cooperative and collaborative activities. She understands that social learning is active, engaged learning and that many students need that extra touch of support and recognition to be successful.

This is a book that can be useful to teachers from kindergarten though middle school. The techniques and activities are that broad in their scope and application. I cannot imagine being a teacher and not having a resource like this at my fingertips. So my advice to fellow teachers is to get the book and get busy engaging your students in ways you never thought possible.

P. David Pearson

CONTENTS

CONTENTS

CONTENTS

CONTENTS

CONTENTS

CONTENTS

STRATEGIES ORGANIZED BY COMPREHENSION STRAND

	Page No.	Summarize	Infer	Determine Importance	Question	Connect	Sensory Imaging	Synthesize
Chapter 2: Conversations About Books	12							
Partner Read and Think	16	✓	✓		✓			
My Partner Said …	20	✓		✓				
I Remember!	22	✓		✓				
Say Something	26		✓		✓			
Book Reviews	28			✓				✓
Alphaboxes: A Reflective Strategy	30	✓	✓	✓				
Two-Word Strategy	32		✓					
Inference Equation	36		✓			✓		✓
In the Text/I Can Infer … Charts	39	✓	✓	✓				✓
Understanding a Character and Hot Seat	41		✓	✓				✓
The Character and Me	42			✓		✓		
V.I.P. ("Very Important Points")	44	✓		✓		✓		
Stimulating Discussion Through Questions	46		✓		✓	✓		
Book Commercials	50	✓						✓
Memorable Moments	52			✓		✓		✓
Drawing Conclusions	53		✓					
Maybe	54		✓					✓
Analyzing Poetry	56						✓	
Get Real	57							✓
Have a Book Party	58							✓
Chapter 3: Oral Retelling	70							
Preparing for a Retell	77	✓		✓				
Retelling Checklist for Fiction	78	✓		✓		✓		
Illustrating the Story	79	✓					✓	
Three-Circle Map	80	✓					✓	
What Is Important?	82	✓	✓	✓				✓
Partner Retelling	84	✓		✓				
Novel Reflections	87	✓		✓	✓			✓
Team Retelling	88	✓						
Spin a Story	91	✓						
Paper Bag Theatre	94	✓		✓			✓	

STRATEGIES ORGANIZED BY COMPREHENSION STRAND

STRATEGIES ORGANIZED BY COMPREHENSION STRAND

	Page No.	Summarize	Infer	Determine Importance	Question	Connect	Sensory Imaging	Synthesize
Chapter 5: Informational Text	166							
Word Prediction	177		✓		✓	✓		
Read, Cover, Remember, Retell	174	✓		✓				
Coding Strategy	176	✓	✓	✓	✓	✓		
Weave a Web of Understanding	178	✓		✓				
Student-Created Dictionaries	179	✓						✓
Information Equation	180	✓	✓	✓		✓		✓
Questioning	182				✓			
Fact or Fib?	184				✓			
Test-Style Questions	186	✓	✓	✓	✓	✓		✓
Magic Jigsaw: A Questioning Strategy	188	✓	✓	✓	✓	✓		
Focusing on Important Ideas	190	✓		✓				
Sum It Up	191	✓		✓				
Reflecting on Main Ideas	192			✓				✓
Nonfiction Scaffold	193	✓						
Drawing Conclusions	194		✓					✓
Generalization Strategy	195		✓	✓				
Leads, Middles, Endings!	196						✓	✓
Preparing an Informational Retell	197	✓		✓				
Table of Contents Retell	198	✓			✓			
Retelling Expository Text	199	✓						
Book Evaluation	200							✓
Investigating Visual Supports	201						✓	✓
Reciprocal Teaching	202	✓		✓	✓	✓		
Alpha Antics	204					✓		✓
Alliteration Fun	206						✓	
A Definition Poem	208	✓		✓			✓	
Research Plan	209	✓						✓
Investigations	210			✓			✓	✓

STRATEGIES ORGANIZED BY CLASSIFICATION OF THINKING

	R. Marzano's Classification of Thinking Skills	Verbs Related to This Classification	Sample Tasks or Questions	L. Hoyt's Strategies That Support This Classification	Page No.
Basic-Level Thinking Skills	**Knowing** (defining, recall)	List, name, label, recall, identify, match, choose, formulate questions, clarify information, observe, store information for recall	• Name the strategies good readers use to understand what they read. • Identify strategies that you use during reading to help you remember content. • Formulate a question about the habitat of a _____.	• Partner Read and Think • I Remember! • Alphabox • V.I.P. Strategy • Stimulating Discussion Through Questions • Partner Retelling • Key Word Strategy • Riddling Along • Read, Cover, Remember, Retell • Coding Strategy • Weave a Web of Understanding • Test-Style Questions • Sum It Up • Reflecting on Main Ideas • Table of Contents Retell • Reciprocal Teaching	16 22 30 44 46 84 130 154 174 176 178 186 191 192 198 202
	Organizing (arranging information)	Categorize, group, classify, compare, contrast, sequence, represent (change the form but not the substance)	• Which fix-up strategies do good readers use when they come to a challenging word? • List the strategies that help you to visualize as you read. Which strategies help you to identify important ideas? • Compare the life cycle of a butterfly with that of a moth.	• Alphabox • The Character and Me • Book Commercials • Maybe • Team Retelling • Spin a Story • Spicing It Up with Line Drawings • Image Search • Writing Letters • Key Word Strategy, group in meaningful clusters • Organizing a Summary • Dual Bio Poems • Coding Strategy • Student-Created Dictionaries • Information Equation • Test-Style Questions • Sum It Up • Reflecting on Main Ideas • Nonfiction Scaffold • Investigations	30 42 50 54 88 91 98 122 129 130 135 156 176 179 180 186 191 192 193 210
Mid- to Upper-Level Thinking Skills	**Applying** (demonstrating prior knowledge in a new situation, transfer of strategy to a new context)	Apply, make, show, record, construct, demonstrate, solve a problem, illustrate, describe how you applied . . .	• What did you do in this text when you got confused? • Describe how you used the V.I.P. strategy to identify important points. • Show how you can use the _____ strategy in two different books.	• **All Strategies:** Each strategy applied in multiple contexts and settings **Also:** • Interactive Journals • Creating a Readers Theatre Script • Riddling Along • Word Prediction • Coding Strategy • Information Equation • Test-Style Questions • Magic Jigsaw • Focusing on Important Ideas • Preparing an Informational Retell • Alliteration Fun • Research Plan	 126 144 154 172 176 180 186 188 190 197 206 209

This table is organized around the "Classifications of Thinking" by Robert J. Marzano.

	R. Marzano's Classification of Thinking Skills	Verbs Related to This Classification	Sample Tasks or Questions	L. Hoyt's Strategies That Support This Classification	Page No.
Mid- to Upper-Level Thinking Skills	**Analyzing** (clarifying information, identifying relationships, and establishing a hierarchy of key ideas)	Outline, diagram, differentiate, analyze, examine relationships, identify characteristics and patterns, main idea, determine importance	• What kind of text requires the most frequent use of fix up strategies for you as a reader? • Which strategies are you most comfortable using? Which ones do you need more practice in applying? • Outline the main ideas in this selection.	• Say Something • Alphabox, to describe a character • Two-Word Strategy • Understanding a Character • The Character and Me • V.I.P. Strategy • Three-Circle Map • Novel Reflections • If I Were the Author • Interactive Journals • Key Word Strategy • Sketch to Stretch • Coding Strategy • Information Equation • Questioning • Test-Style Questions • Focusing on Important Ideas • Preparing an Informational Retell • Investigating Visual Supports • Alliteration Fun	26 30 32 41 42 44 80 87 116 126 130 148 176 180 182 186 190 197 201 206
	Generating (producing new understandings by inferring, predicting, or elaborating)	Conclude, predict, explain, elaborate by adding details or examples, infer, produce new information	• What would happen if a reader never used the fix-up strategy of rereading? • What are the advantages of knowing a range of strategies to help you remember and understand what you read? • Predict five words that you expect to see in this passage on _____. • Explain how you solved this problem.	• Partner Read and Think • My Partner Said … • Two-Word Strategy • In the Text/I Can Infer … Charts • Stimulating Discussion Through Questions • Drawing Conclusions • Maybe • Team Retelling • Spin a Story • Storytelling Glove, with details and opinions • Interactive Journals • Key Word Strategy • My Character Says • Story Reflections • Sketch to Stretch • Word Theatre • Word Prediction • Read, Cover, Remember, Retell • Weave a Web of Understanding • Information Equation • Test-Style Questions • Magic Jigsaw • Generalization Strategy • Reciprocal Teaching • Alliteration Fun • A Definition Poem	16 20 32 39 46 53, 194 54 88 91 96 126 130 138 139 148 150 172 174 178 180 186 188 195 202 206 208

This table is organized around the "Classifications of Thinking" by Robert J. Marzano.

continues on next page

	R. Marzano's Classification of Thinking Skills	Verbs Related to This Classification	Sample Tasks or Questions	L. Hoyt's Strategies That Support This Classification	Page No.
Upper-Level Thinking Skills	**Integrating** (connecting and combining information to summarize and create cohesive statements)	Connect and combine information, summarize into cohesive statements, imagine, generalize, restructure	• Imagine you were reading a book with a stain on the page, covering several words. What could you do to make sense of the text? • Imagine that you were giving advice to a younger student on reading for meaning. Which strategies would you most encourage that younger student to use? • Summarize your learning from this passage.	• My Partner Said ... • I Remember! • Say Something • Alphabox, words used in retell or writing • Inference Equation • V.I.P. Strategy • Drawing Conclusions • Analyzing Poetry • Retelling Checklist for Fiction • Three-Circle Map • Novel Reflections • Retells on Tape • Book Rating and Book Review • Interactive Journals • Key Word Strategy • Story Reflections • Sketch to Stretch • Personal Narrative • Read, Cover, Remember, Retell • Coding Strategy • Weave a Web of Understanding • Student-Created Dictionaries • Information Equation • Fact or Fib? • Test-Style Questions • Nonfiction Scaffold • Preparing an Informational Retell • Retelling Expository Text • A Definition Poem • Investigations	20 22 26 30 36 44 53, 194 56 78 80 87 98 118 126 130 139 148 157 174 176 178 179 180 184 186 193 197 199 208 210

This table is organized around the "Classifications of Thinking" by Robert J. Marzano.

	R. Marzano's Classification of Thinking Skills	Verbs Related to This Classification	Sample Tasks or Questions	L. Hoyt's Strategies That Support This Classification	Page No.
Upper-Level Thinking Skills	**Evaluating** (assessing quality, verifying importance, considering accuracy, establishing criteria)	Judge, evaluate, rate, verify, assess, define criteria	• Which fix-up strategy is the most important to learn? Explain why you think so. • Which comprehension strategies have you found to be most helpful? Why? • If we were to create a rubric for a high-quality piece of descriptive writing, what should be on the list? • Evaluate the verb choices in the book _____.	• Say Something, focused on evaluation • Book Reviews • Two-Word Strategy • V.I.P. Strategy, partners reaching consensus on most important points • Stimulating Discussion Through Questions • Get Real • What is Important? • Partner Retelling • Compare and Contrast • Retells on Tape • If I Were the Author • Book Rating • Image Search • Key Word Strategy • Attribute Graph • Character Analysis • Coding Strategy • Fact or Fib? • Test-Style Questions • Generalization Strategy • Leads, Middles, Endings! • Preparing an Informational Retell • Book Evaluation • Investigating Visual Supports • Writing self-assessment **Also:** • Create your own rubrics • Read two selections on the same topic and compare author style, point of view, content • Use self-assessment strategies • Create lists such as Attributes of a Great Reader or Attributes of a Great Personal Narrative	26 28 32 44 46 57 82 84 97 98 116 118 122 130 146 153 176 184 186 195 196 197 200 201 224

This table is organized around the "Classifications of Thinking" by Robert J. Marzano.

ACKNOWLEDGMENTS

The Researchers

P. David Pearson, Nell Duke, and Bob Marzano shared the gift of their time and enormous expertise to review this work, affirm the rock-solid research base, and lend their support. They have always had my deepest respect. I add my sincere appreciation.

The Review Team

We asked elementary and middle school educators from around the country to help us reflect on the original edition of *Revisit, Reflect, Retell* and share their thinking about the strategies that have been sure-fire winners with students. They were also invited to offer suggestions for new features that might help this resource be even more useful to teachers and learners. The responses of this team helped us to bring new shape and vision to this resource, as well as affirming our belief that the content was already solid, and worthy of a fresh new face. Our sincere thanks to Marlene Hill, Mattie Fallen, Jan McCall, Glenda Haley, Kelly Boswell, Kelly Davis, Sally Wells, Jennifer Gotkin, Sonja Parks, Ceretha Mitchell, Marie Puett, Debbie McMahan, Denise Lutkin, and Jacquelyne Vereen for their thoughtful responses and support.

The Permissions and Photographic Team

Readers put out the call for more photographs and visuals to support the strategies described in *Revisit, Reflect, Retell*. Teresa Therriault, Marie Govro, Leah Starkovich, Sarah Phillips, Lory Lauridsen, Sonja Parks, April Willard, Kelly Davis, Barbara Coleman, Ceretha Mitchell, Barbara Petruccio, Marlene Hill, Mattie Fallen, Sandy Gordon, Mandy Caine, Carol Updegraff, Jeanne Yttreness, and Jan McCall came forward in amazing ways. Special thanks go to Gilbert Park Elementary in Portland, Oregon; the schools of Davidson County, North Carolina; Wingate Elementary in Monroe, North Carolina; Hudson City Schools in Hudson, Ohio; Fort Belvoir School in Fairfax County, Virginia; Kinnaman Elementary in Beaverton, Oregon; and Central Schools in Independence, Oregon. These forward-thinking educators opened their hearts and their learning environments to help us celebrate this new edition with visuals designed to empower teachers and showcase readers and writers at work. They helped us to track down parent permissions for photographs, student work samples, video footage, and so much more. Their role in the development of the updated version of *Revisit* was essential and very much appreciated.

ACKNOWLEDGMENTS

Team Heinemann

They are trusted professionals who bring art and craft together in the beautiful and educationally responsible books they publish. It has been an honor to again work with this incredible team of experts and friends. Abby Heim led the way with production while Maura Sullivan anchored my work with her insights, thoughtful editing, and mastery of the marketing world.

The project team at Heinemann also includes (first and foremost!) Stephanie Turner, editorial coordinator; Denise Botelho, copyeditor; Jenny Jensen Greenleaf, cover and page designer; Gina Poirier, typesetter and page designer; Pat Carls, marketing director; Eric Chalek, copywriter; Roberta Lew, rights, permissions, and contracts supervisor; Steve Bernier, senior manufacturing buyer; Nicole Russell, CD technology coordinator and designer; and Kevin Carlson, video coordinator.

Bill Miller

Bill, thank you for creating the video clips that bring some of these strategies to life. Your friendship, artistry, and amazing ability to listen have helped me more than you know.

Setting the Stage

How to Scaffold for Deep Engagement

Set the Stage for Comprehension

Just as the director and designer create a stage setting that helps the audience understand and connect to a dramatic performance, teachers must create the environments in which students are challenged to read a wide range of texts deeply and thoughtfully. With the goal of deep thinking, teachers in this kind of learning environment invite responses and reactions, and stretch students' thinking to levels of reflection they might not reach on their own. The culture of learning is one of respect in which teachers and learners are partners who say things like this to one another:

- *If we look at this from another perspective . . .*
- *Can you think of an example from the text to support our thinking?*
- *Have you considered . . . ?*

- *What strategies best helped you to understand this selection?*
- *Can you cite a specific place in the text where this strategy helped you understand?*

When the stage is set for deep comprehension and engagement, there is a sense of commitment and energy that drives learners to explore, wonder, and understand with greater depth. This elevated state of engagement is supported by three distinct levels of responses that include efferent, aesthetic, and critical/analytical. *Efferent responses*, often referred to as *literal comprehension*, engage readers in unpacking the facts on a page or taking in the sequence of events in a story. *Aesthetic responses* invite reactions, opinions, connections, or questions about the content and craft. This level of response engages readers at an emotional level. *Critical/analytical responses*, sometimes described as *critical literacy*, are those in which the reader challenges a text, an author, the premise behind the work, the validity of the content, or the purpose of the piece. In this level, readers look beyond the text, considering points of view, the author's intent, cultural references, or bias. When all three levels of responses are utilized to scaffold reflective reading, readers expand their view of the text by examining, reacting to, and analyzing the selection (Pearson 2008).

> **LEVELS OF RESPONSE**
> - **Efferent: The information (facts) readers extract from the text.**
> - **Aesthetic: Expressive responses that invite learners to share their thinking.**
> - **Critical/analytical: Readers interrogate the text, the author, the issue, and the purpose.**

Teach Strategies Explicitly

In setting the stage for comprehension, teachers explicitly model how good readers reach into a text, cracking open the thinking processes of an expert reader in a way that students can replicate. They explicitly demonstrate strategies and tools readers use to record their thinking, exposing their thinking and their written responses in a highly visual way that students can follow as a model for their own thinking and writing.

Transfer Responsibility

Students first observe the teacher modeling how to use a strategy, a learning tool, or a process. Then, student partners replicate the actions of the teacher while he or she coaches on the sidelines. Once the teacher is sure that the processes and procedures of a strategy or learning task are clearly understood, individual students apply their learning independently.

At each level of implementation the teacher guides students to consider:

- *What did I learn?*
- *What are my thoughts about this topic, this selection, this author, and so on?*
- *What strategies best helped me to understand?*
- *Which next steps will best support my work as a reader, a thinker, and a writer?*

Most important, the teacher takes the vital importance of explicit modeling very seriously. Teresa Therriault, co-author of *Mastering the Mechanics* (Hoyt and Therriault 2008), writes:

> As educators, we should never ask students to do something they haven't seen us do first.

When teachers explicitly model strategies and learning tasks, students are empowered with the language of deep thinking. They have higher expectations for their own reflections, and they have a clear picture of how to approach each learning task.

> **At the heart of deep comprehension is a teacher who engages in explicit modeling and coaching. Assignments are given after students observe the teacher actively applying the target learning.**

In Kamehameha School in Honolulu, Linda thinks aloud and explicitly models the processes she expects students to use, then shows students how to engage with an In the Text/I Can Infer chart

Create Walls That Teach

The walls of a comprehension classroom are not areas to be "decorated." Rather, they are tools for learning. They should tell a story of strategy use and reflective thinking, making visible to all that strategy and reflection are savored and supported across all areas of the curriculum. Walls that support comprehension and lift students to deeper thinking might display:

- lists of processes used by readers and writers
- quotations from master writers

- work samples that inspire students to reach higher as readers, writers, and critical thinkers

- lists of questions reading partners could ask each other

Posters that the teacher and students have created together list the strategies that have been explored. Anchor charts itemize the steps readers use in applying the strategy. Work samples show how the strategies have been effectively applied. Students, teachers, and parents are able to identify areas of curricular emphasis just by looking at the wall.

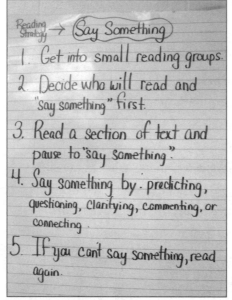

This Say Something chart posted at Tyro Middle School reminds students of the steps in applying the strategy.

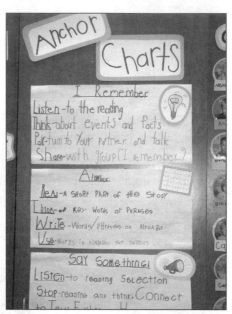

Students at Welcome Elementary created these charts to celebrate and support their strategy use.

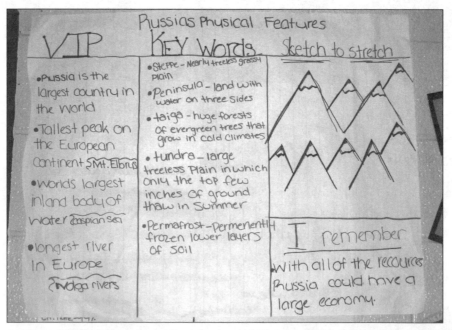

At Brown Middle School, students synthesize their understanding of Russia's physical features using a range of strategies including V.I.P., Key Word, Sketch to Stretch, and I Remember.

Engage Readers In Powerful Conversations

> *Comprehension improves when we engage students in rich discussions that allow students to integrate knowledge, experience, strategies, and textual insights.*
>
> (P. David Pearson 2008)

When we open the door to real dialogue and genuine conversation, we create a sense of celebration around the wide range of responses students have to the same text. We create the expectation that conversations are filled with accountable, relevant considerations of learning, that opinions are encouraged, and that thinking is supported with evidence from the text. Students are encouraged to share their responses but also to justify their thinking. The goal is to learn to interrogate the text, the author, and the issues.

At Kinnaman Elementary in Beaverton, Oregon, Pat Webb guides students in using the text to support and justify reflections and deep thinking.

Float Learning on a Sea of Talk

Historically, conversations in classrooms have been teacher controlled. The teacher asks a question. Students' hands are raised. One student responds. This type of interactional pattern results in very few learners getting to speak and produces a sluggish attitude about comprehension: struggling learners quickly learn that if they are quiet long enough, a more verbal peer will speak out and provide a response.

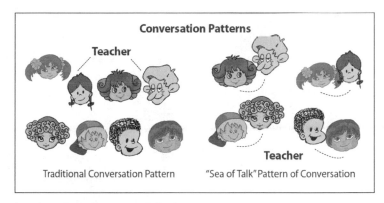

Conversation Patterns

Teacher

Traditional Conversation Pattern

Teacher

"Sea of Talk" Pattern of Conversation

When the pattern of interaction shifts to a *distributed discourse model*, the teacher still poses questions, but students do not raise their hands or try to get the attention of the teacher. Instead, students respond to the question by having a literate conversation with a "thinking partner." Because *all* students must now interact with the question, cognition is distributed and more students engage with the learning (Resnick 1991, Allington 2007).

Accountable talk between partners lifts learning and increases engagement.

> *Partner conversations support and encourage language use for all students.*

Create Contexts in Which Students *Use* Academic Language and Vocabulary

Another benefit of distributed discourse is that students have a rich and authentic context in which they can immediately *use* the academic language they are learning. This helps them gain control over concepts and vocabulary. The immediate use of vocabulary, framed within a conversational setting, supports differentiation and is particularly powerful for English language learners. For example, in the following science lesson on volcanoes:

1. The teacher creates an anchor chart showing the flow of magma and labels the core elements of the volcanic structure.

2. Thinking partners select three words that they think are most critical to their study of volcanoes.

3. Partners justify their selections with supporting statements.

4. Partners record the words they have identified as most important in their learning logs and prepare to share with another team.

The result: All students are engaged with the target academic vocabulary as readers, as language users, and as writers. They have engaged in the important comprehension-seeking strategy of determining importance. Their learning has *floated on a sea of talk*, lifting their control over both language and content to a higher level (Britton 1992).

The process works equally well in kindergarten.

Scaffold and Support Accountable Conversations

Partner talk isn't likely to be effective without coaching so it's important to *show* students what accountable conversations look like and sound like. They need to learn to face one another physically, maintain eye contact, and contribute ideas that extend and deepen understanding.

To model such a conversation, I ask a student or another teacher to serve as my thinking partner and we sit together while the rest of the class gathers around us. Before my partner and I begin our discussion, I challenge observers to listen carefully, noticing the way we look each other in the eye, acknowledge and extend each other's ideas, and always treat each other with respect.

The author and Carol Updegraff at Hopland Elementary in Ukiah, California, model a partner conversation for students.

After the demonstration, the students and I create a chart listing the attributes of a thinking partner conversation (see the example in Figure 1–1). This chart is then posted where students can refer to it as they conduct and fine-tune their conversations.

Accountable Conversation

What Does It Look Like?	What Does It Sound Like?
We maintain eye contact.	*I see what you're saying . . .*
We nod our heads.	*Great point. I am also wondering . . .*
Our bodies are turned toward each other.	*Can you say more about that?*

FIGURE 1–1 *Accountable Conversation*

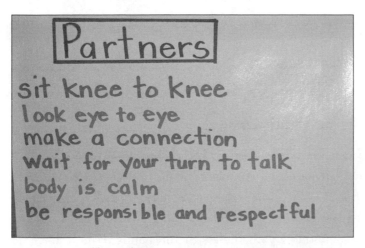

Partners
sit knee to knee
look eye to eye
make a connection
wait for your turn to talk
body is calm
be responsible and respectful

Students at Wallburg Elementary created this list of Partner Turn and Talk reminders to help lift the quality of accountable talk.

Some students benefit from a list of conversation starters to help them launch partner conversations. To support those students, I often make a poster listing stems such as those that follow. This poster changes and grows as students gain proficiency and learn how to lift one another to deeper levels of thinking.

Stems to Start a Discussion

I wonder...	An important point was...
I noticed...	I realized...
I liked...	I think...
I feel...	The selection made me think of...
I can infer...	If I could change something, I would...
My favorite part was...	The author's purpose may be...

Turn, Talk, and *Listen*

Partner conversations are often referred to as a *Turn and Talk*, but the real emphasis should be on active listening and shared responsibility for committed engagement with the topic. Michael Opitz (2006) reminds us that active listening is too often ignored as a learning tool. We need to teach students that part of their responsibility in a conversation is to be a thoughtful, reflective listener who can connect with, extend, and elaborate on the ideas of another speaker. Partner pairs who are actively listening say things like:

- *Tell me more about your thinking on that . . .*
- *What led you to that line of thinking?*
- *What did you notice in the text that supports your idea?*
- *I can "link up" to that thought . . .*
- *You comment makes me wonder . . .*
- *Your comment reminds me that . . .*
- *What did you think about . . .*

Model Quality Thinking and Listening

To help learners become knowledgeable speakers and active listeners, we need to model invitational language that stimulates quality conversation and deep thinking (see Figure 1–2). When we use language that invites deeper thinking and display that language on charts so students can refer to it easily, the students become more comfortable with these structures and are more likely to utilize them during their partner conversations.

Invitations to Deeper Conversation

Can someone say that in another way?

Who can elaborate on what was just said?

Please explain what led you to this thought.

Can you support your thinking with evidence from the text?

Can someone see another viewpoint here?

What are the main ideas in this selection?

What do you notice about this relationship?

What is significant about the behavior of this character?

How might this problem best be solved?

If we were to design a test on this selection, what questions should be included?

What are the most important ideas here?

What are your questions? What are you wondering?

Can someone summarize the point that was just made?

What conclusions can we draw?

How might this compare with…?

If we were to evaluate this, what should we consider?

What perspective has the author taken with this topic?

How might we verify the accuracy of this?

What criteria does it appear the author used in saying…?

What might the author want us to believe?

FIGURE 1–2

Build the Expectation That Readers Often Write About Their Reading

When we write about what we've read, we reflect on and solidify our learning. We are challenged to review and synthesize our understandings and consider how our new learning relates to our prior knowledge. In a reflective classroom, students know that they will be asked to write in response to their reading—to consider both the content they encountered and the strategies they used to develop as a reader or a writer. With this mind-set, students anticipate written responses while they read, using sticky notes to jot down key ideas or list questions that may inform their reflections.

> *What did I learn? How did this strategy support my learning? What was memorable in this selection?*

Students increase their metacognitive awareness when they reflect on their learning and consider ways in which their learning may influence their interaction with another text.

When readers write about their learning, they engage in deeper levels of reflection and remember more of the content.

Read, Read, Read

Volume Counts

It is well proven that reading volume, the amount of time spent reading connected texts, is directly linked to achievement (Allington 2006, Elly 1992, Cipielewski and Stanovich 1992). Just as concert musicians and Olympic athletes dedicate enormous amounts of time to practicing their craft, students need to read thousands of words in meaningful texts every day. As we set the stage for deep thinking, we need to consider how much time students spend reading accessible texts. Richard

Allington (2006) suggests ninety minutes a day at a minimum, with the caution that the time be spent reading real books, not participating in reading-related activities. Solving acrostics, filling in the blanks, coloring illustrations, and similar activities must be set aside to make room for the vast amount of reading that students need to do to reach higher levels of comprehension.

Shelley Harwayne (2002) reminds us to treat every instructional minute as a *precious pearl*. With that metaphor as a guide, it is easier to let go of projects and activities that qualify as fun but offer little credibility in furthering learning. "Activities" must not eat up valuable minutes that could be spent getting lost in a story or thinking critically about an informational text.

> *Set the stage by carefully considering reading volume and assuring that all students, especially those who struggle, spend at least ninety minutes a day reading selections that capture their interest and their sense of wonder.*

It is essential to remember that reading deeply is the priority. Learning experiences that take time away from reading should be carefully selected as tools for lifting learning, rather than filling time.

Many Types of Text on Many Subjects

As you set the stage for increasing reading volume, it is also essential to consider ways to increase the breadth of text types that students encounter. Because comprehension development has been found to be genre specific (Duke 2003), students must be exposed to a wide range of genres and formats in both fiction and informational texts. Primary students should be reading a balance of 50 percent fiction and 50 percent nonfiction. Upper-elementary and middle school students should be reading an average of 30 percent fiction and 70 percent nonfiction to ensure development is broad and deep. With this platform of diverse text types, reader explorations of efferent, aesthetic, and critical/analytical responses become cross-curricular experiences that stimulate comprehension across the widest possible range of text types.

> *Comprehension cannot be developed in fiction alone. It must be carefully nurtured and supported across a wide range of text types.*

CHAPTER 2 AT-A-GLANCE

Retelling Strategy	Comprehension Strands	Classification of Thinking	Page
Partner Read and Think	Question	Knowing	16
	Infer	Generating	
	Summarize	Integrating	
My Partner Said…	Summarize	Knowing	20
	Determine importance	Generating	
		Integrating	
I Remember!	Summarize	Knowing	22
	Determine importance	Generating	
		Integrating	
Say Something	Question	Analyzing	26
	Infer	Integrating	
Book Reviews	Synthesize	Organizing	28
	Determine importance	Evaluating	
Alphaboxes: A Reflective Strategy	Summarize	Knowing	30
	Determine importance	Organizing	
		Analyzing	
Two-Word Strategy	Infer	Analyzing	32
		Generating	
		Integrating	
Inference Equation	Infer	Generating	36
	Synthesize	Integrating	
In the Text/I Can Infer…Charts	Infer	Generating	39
	Determine importance	Summarizing	
	Synthesize	Generating	
Understanding a Character and Hot Seat	Infer	Analyzing	41
	Synthesize	Generating	
The Character and Me	Determine importance	Organizing	42
	Connect	Analyzing	
V.I.P. ("Very Important Points")	Summarize	Knowing	44
	Determine importance	Analyzing	
	Connect	Evaluating	
Stimulating Discussion Through Questions	Question	Knowing	46
	Infer	Generating	
	Connect	Evaluating	
Book Commercials	Summarize	Applying	50
	Synthesize	Organizing	
Memorable Moments	Synthesize	Analyze	52
		Evaluate	
Drawing Conclusions	Infer	Generating	53
Maybe	Infer	Generating	54
	Synthesize	Integrating	
		Organizing	
Analyzing Poetry	Use sensory imaging	Integrating	56
Get Real	Synthesize	Evaluating	57
Have a Book Party	Synthesize	Evaluating	58
		Integrating	

Conversations About Books

Personal and Social Explorations of Meaning

At one time, quiet classrooms were considered the ideal environment for learning. However, as research has demonstrated the social nature of learning, we must remember that it is essential to provide opportunities for children to talk about what they are learning and the strategies they are using for inquiry (Braunger and Lewis 2006). These questions and dialogue need to be genuine acts of communication and not simply a rote reaction to situations controlled by an adult (Peterson and Eeds 2006). Through in-depth, authentic conversations in which children are encouraged to share their opinions and understandings, we can help children to delve more deeply as thinkers, clarify ideas, and verify information.

There is a strong and important link between oral language and reading comprehension (Clay 1972; Wilson and Cleland 1985). Sharing and comparing through the oral mode of communication demands that the learner activate understanding of a story. Together, through conversation, readers can

consider the potential meaning of a passage, clarifying their thoughts and reflecting on the processes that help them to create meaning while reading (Hoyt 2003). Through dialogue, readers measure their own understandings against the perceptions of others, consider the quality of their understanding, examine diverse perspectives, and make internal adjustments in their reading. In each exchange, oral language proficiency is bolstered and expanded, elaborated upon and stretched.

Through a long history of working with children who are challenged by learning, I find that these children in particular benefit from conversation. Traditional comprehension questions focus attention on the teacher rather than the text and cast the learner in a passive rather than an active role. Cambourne's Conditions of Learning make it clear that we must increase learner responsibility if we are to increase learning. Conversations and genuine dialogue place responsibility directly in the hands of the learner. Challenged learners who engage regularly in rigorous conversations about texts begin to anticipate engagement in meaningful dialogue and engage in more-intensive monitoring of their own comprehension.

The challenge we face is how to create an environment in which conversations stay focused on the text *and* assist children in connecting their world knowledge with the text being discussed.

Questions for Students to Ask Each Other About Books

What did you notice?

What did you like?

What is your opinion?

What did you wonder?

What does this mean?

What did you learn?

How did it make you feel?

What parts of the story seemed especially important to you?

As you read, were there any places where you thought of yourself, people you know, or experiences you have had?

Were there any parts you especially liked?

What did you read that makes you think that?

What do you know that you didn't know before?

Were there any parts you would have changed if you were the author?

What do you think the author did especially well?

What is the strongest literary element?

Questions for Students to Ask Each Other About Being a Reader

How did you function as a learner?

What did you do well?

What did you do to help yourself as a reader?

What strategies did you use most in this book?

- read on to check for meaning
- thought about what made sense
- reread to regain meaning
- used picture clues
- broke unknown words into chunks

What challenged you as a reader?

Are there any adjustments you need to make in your reading?

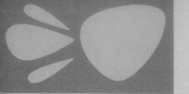

Partner Read and Think

VIEW THIS STRATEGY IN ACTION ON THE DVD.

Partner Read and Think is based on the research that so effectively supports reciprocal teaching, but it requires fewer social skills as it is completed by partners instead of teams of four. The process engages partners in applying six distinct steps to each segment of text that is read. The combination of steps helps students engage at several levels of comprehension and encourages language use as partners navigate a selection.

Partner Read and Think guides partner pairs in:

* placing a stop sign

* predicting words they think are likely to appear

* reading the section (silently or in unison)

* identifying words they find interesting or are confused about

* summarizing the learning.

Model

I like using an enlarged text or a text projected on an overhead projector when modeling the steps of this strategy to ensure that students can clearly see the text as I am modeling.

* Students watch as I place a sticky note stop sign in the text. During a Partner Read and Think, it is important to complete all steps before moving the stop sign to the next chunk of text.

Explicitly show students how to place sticky notes on the text as a reminder to apply all steps in a short passage before reading on.

Partner Read and Think

Comprehension Strands	Level of Thinking	Action Verbs
Question	Knowing	Formulate a question
Infer	Generating	Predict
Summarize	Integrating	Summarize

* Next, I show them how I scan quickly across the text and predict words that I think are likely to appear. This is an essential step in bringing out academic vocabulary that will support understanding.

During Word Prediction, students activate prior knowledge about the topic and focus on key academic vocabulary.

* I then read the section aloud or have students join me in reading the section in unison.

Use a Literacy Frame to model selection of "an interesting word."

* For the next step, I use a Literacy Frame as originally designed by Don Holdaway to direct student attention to words I think are worthy of attention. The frame should be proportioned to match the text you are reading so the words fit inside the frame. For student-size texts and use at the overhead, guidelines for making a

frame appear on page 18. For big books, use the pattern as a guide then enlarge the frame to fit around the words in your favorite big books.

* The next step is to model asking questions and wondering aloud about the words, the visuals, or the concepts. Questions are important because they encourage readers to interact with the selection.

Notice that the words appear in a Literacy Frame, then are also written on sticky notes to make them more visible to students.

* Finally, I model a brief summary to show students how I can sum up my learning before I move the sticky note and proceed to the next section of the reading.

Kay and Will think together as they navigate a newsmagazine.

Students in Mandy Caine's third grade created bookmarks to support Partner Read and Think experiences.

1. Place a stop sign.

2. Predict.

3. Read together.

4. Find interesting words.

5. Ask questions.

 I wonder...

6. Summarize.

I learned that
_____

Literacy Frames

Step 1: Fold a long, thin piece of paper or oak tag in half. Cut (and save) a strip from the middle (shaded section). Then staple together (one staple) the open ends of the large piece.

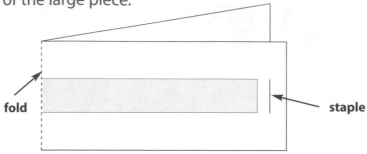

Step 2: Slip one side of the folded strip (removed in Step 1) into the Literacy Frame, stapling it at the bottom after insertion. The staples prevent the slider from falling out of the frame.

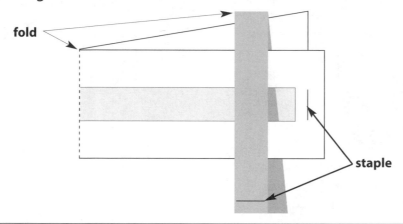

Frames should be made with windows sized to match the print you are reading:

Primary-level reading

The dog ran in.

Intermediate-level reading

The puppy dashed into the house.

FIGURE 2–1: *Literacy Frames. See the photographs at the top of page 17 for examples of the literacy frame in use.*

Partner Read and Think

1. **Place a stop sign.**

2. **Predict words.**

3. **Read silently or in unison.**

4. **Find interesting words.**

5. **Ask questions.**  I wonder . . .

6. **Summarize.** I learned that _____

My Partner Said...

Step 1: Modeling

Thinking Together

During a whole-class experience, such as an interactive read-aloud, select a student to be your partner and model how you turn and think together each time you pause during the reading. Share ideas and offer reflections, points of view, and opinions while the class listens and observes. Be sure to face your partner so you are showing respect by making eye contact and modeling appropriate body language for the rest of the students.

Select a thinking partner and clearly model expectations for thinking.

Reporting

Students from Hudson, Ohio, meet to share their "My Partner Said..." statements.

After each short conversation, you and your partner need to report your thinking to the group by using the stem, "My Partner Said..." Your goal is to share highlights of the reflections contributed by your partner. It is helpful if you show students how you use your partner's name to be sure the creator of the idea gets full credit.

Examples

My partner, Anna, said that Goldilocks should have been punished for entering the home of the bears without knocking.

My partner, Julio, said that communication during the Civil War must have been extremely difficult because they didn't have telephones, television, or the Internet the way we do today.

Step 2: Guided Practice

Continue the interactive read-aloud and have partner pairs move from thinking together to reporting using the stem, "My Partner Said..." You may need to cue the students to use their partner's name when reporting.

As students gain proficiency, they benefit from doing My Partner Said... in teams of four so every student has more opportunity to report the thinking of his or her partners.

Extend the Learning: Shared Reading

Using a passage projected on the overhead or found in a big book or in a newsmagazine, show the students how to insert sticky notes every few pages or even every few paragraphs. These stickies serve as "stop signs" to remind students to chunk the text to create pauses in their reading. Each stop sign signals time to talk to their thinking partners and then report the ideas their partner has shared.

My Partner Said . . .

Name of reader_____ My partner is _____

We read _____ (reading selection)

Readers,

As you and your partner prepare to use this strategy, place sticky notes at intervals in your reading selection to remind you to stop and think together. Each time you stop, use your best thinking to reflect on what you have read. Then, jot a thought or sketch a quick picture based on the ideas shared by your partner. Your goal is to listen carefully and summarize the thinking of your partner.

My Partner Said . . .

My partner's most important reflection about this selection was _____.

My partner helped me to understand that _____.

I Remember!

I especially like this strategy with informational texts because content can be unpacked so much more easily when students remember to read short amounts, pause to think about what they learned, then interact with the next passage.

Step 1: Modeling

Explain to the students that they are responsible to listen carefully while you read a passage aloud. Their goal is to remember information they find especially interesting or believe to be important. Remind the students to listen and remember, then start a brief read-aloud. I am careful to read a brief passage, then stop and reflect silently. I want students to notice that I take a moment to pause before sharing. Then, I use the stem, "I Remember!" and share what I remember from the page. This sets a clear model for retelling and summarizing.

When teaching the strategy, read short passages then have students turn and say, "I Remember!"

Step 2: Guided Practice

As students catch on to the process, I challenge them to share I Remember! points with a thinking partner each time I stop reading.

Note: If the content is loaded with new concepts and new vocabulary, read very short amounts between each stopping point. If the content is based on well-known material and topics, you may be able to read longer passages without sacrificing content retention.

Step 3: Independent Practice

Partners read silently, then give each other a thumbs-up each time they reach a stopping point and are ready to share their I Remember! reflections.

Extend the Learning

✳ Weave the I Remember! strategy into small-group instruction, science and social studies content studies, mathematics, and even into independent reading. To scaffold independence, I give students sticky notes and ask them to place them at stopping points through their text. If the content is dense, I might suggest they create stopping points after every paragraph or at the end of every page to ensure that they can control the volume of information.

✳ Write! Writing is a logical next step. Since students stop so often to share I Remember! comments with a partner, they have a high level of control over the academic vocabulary of the topic and are able to write about what they have learned.

I learned that the tadpole grows gills but When the tadpole turn into a froglet the gills close up and the grow lungs. the froglets can go up to the land but not for long since the have thin skin they can't stay up to long or the skin will dryout.

Kala M.

Kala uses the I Remember! strategy as a springboard to her writing about frogs.

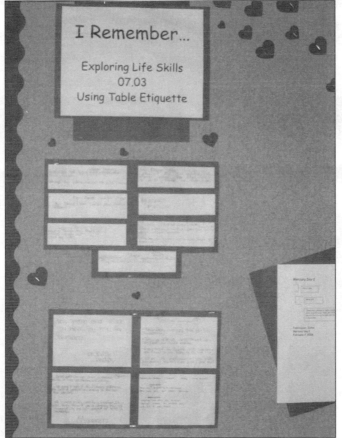

I Remember...

Exploring Life Skills
07.03
Using Table Etiquette

I Remember! was used to support Life Skills Curriculum in a middle school classroom for exceptional children.

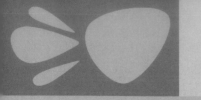

*Students in a middle school technology class use
I Remember! to solidify content understanding.*

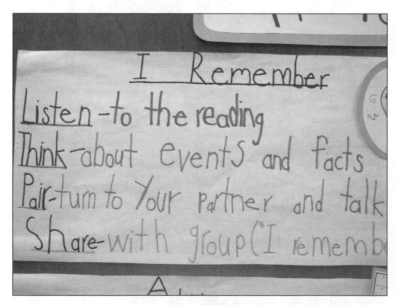

*Students in Davidson County, North Carolina work together to create
I Remember! posters in their own words.*

I Remember!

Reader/Listener _____ Date _____

The Topic _____

Use this box to make a quick sketch about the topic or jot down important words that will help you remember the content.

Write your three most important I Remember! ideas.

1. I remember_____

_____

2. I remember_____

_____

3. I remember_____

_____

Say Something

When readers are always given a set of questions to answer or discussion starters to stimulate conversation, they can become dependent on such structures or—worse yet—develop the notion that conversations about reading are for the teacher rather than for the readers. Say Something is designed to build the expectation that readers talk to each other about their reading, but what they talk about is up to them. They may choose to respond with a prediction, with a thought about how the text relates to a personal experience, or with an opinion.

I find that in the beginning, this works best as a partner activity.

Say Something

Comprehension Strands	Level of Thinking	Action Verbs
Question	Analyzing	Examine relationships, determine importance
Infer	Integrating	Connect, combine

The Process

1. Students meet with a partner. Each partner should have a copy of the same reading material. You might consider using narratives, magazines, news articles, and so on.

2. The partners make an agreement about how they will proceed with their reading. They might choose to read chorally, trade off by paragraphs, or read silently to a chosen stopping point. When they reach the stopping point, each partner needs to Say Something about the reading.

3. Partners return to Step 2 and select another stopping point before reading on.

Students at Welcome Elementary celebrate their learning by writing their Say Something thoughts on the topic.

The Say Something strategy makes it possible for everyone to contribute to conversations as all responses are welcome as long as they are presented in a respectful manner.

Adapted from *Creating Classrooms for Authors,* by Short, Harste, with Burke, Heinemann (1988).

An Alternative

Once students learn the process and become comfortable with the expectation that everyone needs to Say Something, they can try this in a group of three or four. As the group size is enlarged, it is very important to ensure that:

✱ The readers select a method that keeps everyone reading most of the time. They could choose silent reading or unison reading. They might choose readers theatre. They could even try trading paragraphs, but here it would be important to have multiple voices reading each part so that tangled readers don't establish ineffective models of reading and the listeners don't have long to wait for their turn. The goal is to read, so strategies that keep readers actively engaged with print rather than spending time as listeners need to be emphasized.

✱ With a larger group, I have found it helpful to have a structure to ensure that everyone has a chance to Say Something. A cooperative learning technique that works well is having students put their pencils in the center of the table after they contribute a thought. They cannot talk again until all pencils are on the table. This technique builds the expectation that everyone will need to contribute to the conversation and ensures that strong verbal learners do not dominate the discussion.

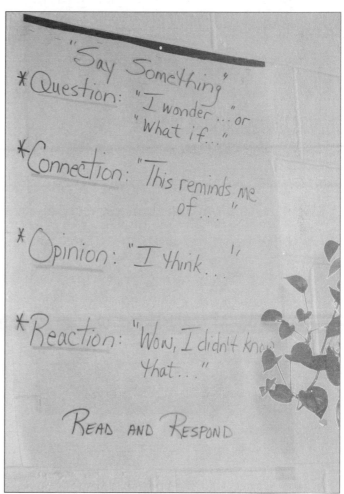

The quality of Say Something responses can be elevated with modeling and charts such as the one created by this middle school class in Davidson County, North Carolina.

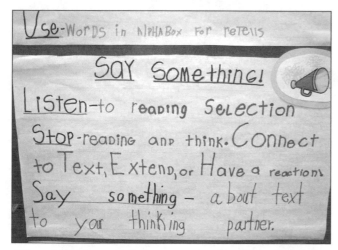

When students create their own posters identifying the strategy steps they use, they have a stronger sense of ownership and are more likely to carry the strategy to independence.

Book Reviews

Book reviews are a quick and easy way to engage students in critical, evaluative thinking. As with all other strategies, I do a think-aloud and reflect aloud as I model for students.

For more proficient students, I would open with a professional book review from the *New York Times*, the newsletters produced by Barnes and Noble or Borders, or one from a local newspaper. Then, I would show them how I would create my own book review of *Harry Potter and the Order of the Phoenix*. Be sure to explain to the students that you will write in a conversational style as if you are talking to someone who is interested in this book. Your goal is to give the next person a window into your response to the selection.

Become a model for critical, evaluative thinking as you evaluate and reflect on books you share with students.

Book Reviews		
Comprehension Strands	**Level of Thinking**	**Action Verbs**
Synthesize	Organizing	Classify
Determine Importance	Evaluating	Judge, evaluate, assess

Example

My think-aloud might sound something like:

I have been thinking that it would be really helpful if we each place a sticky note inside the cover of a book after we have read it. On the sticky note, we could share our thinking about the book and then the next person who picks up the book can take advantage of our evaluation. Rating a book isn't easy. With *Amos and Boris*, the book I just read to you, I know that I appreciate the wonderful vocabulary. I love phrases like *phosphorescent sea* and wonderful words like *illuminate*. If I was only judging this book on vocabulary, I would give it five stars for sure. However, I am also looking at the pictures. They aren't very interesting. A reader needs to really focus on visualizing to get a mental picture with this book. So, I am going to give this book five stars for vocabulary, two stars for art, and four stars for the theme as I think that friendship is one of the most important things in the world. You can rate your books on criteria you select. You might want to rate them for character develop-

Mrs Hoyt's Sticky Note Review
Amos and Boris by William Steig

Vocabulary ☆ ☆ ☆ ☆ ☆

Art ☆ ☆

Theme ☆ ☆ ☆ ☆

I gave this book these ratings because _____

ment, setting, interest, or the ability to draw you into the story. Just remember that these sticky notes aren't very large so you need to pick the most important reflection you can for each book.

Harry Potter Book Review by Carlos

Harry Potter and the Order of the Phoenix is not only the longest Harry Potter book it's also the best. This time the story is scarier and left me wishing I never had to put it down. This book has many exciting plot twists and turns. Even though it's long, I was on the edge of my seat from beginning to end. I would recommend this book to anyone!

5 Stars!!

Sticky note reviews engage even the youngest learners in critical analytical thinking.

Ronald's Sticky Note Review

Alphaboxes: A Reflective Strategy

Alphaboxes are a fun and stimulating way to reflect on a story or a unit of study. After reading, students work in pairs or small groups to think of words that reflect important points in the story. They insert their words into the appropriate alphaboxes on the form, making sure they tell how each selected word related to the story or topic. The result is a lively stretch of vocabulary, a rich network of different perspectives, and a wealth of conversation about the focus story.

Alphaboxes are also a wonderful support system for students of all ages and in all content areas. To get maximum mileage from Alphaboxes, as well as other strategies, give students time to reflect on the tool and consider: What were the steps that I followed in using this tool? How did this tool help me as a learner?

Kindergarten students draw words from their class Alphabox to support their independent writing.

Alphaboxes: A Reflective Strategy

Comprehension Strands	Level of Thinking	Action Verbs
Summarize	Knowing	Label , choose
Determine importance	Organizing	Group, classify
	Analyzing	Describe, identify characteristics, main idea

Extend the Learning

✱ Students who have watched *Jeopardy* on television enjoy writing questions to go with the focus words. For example: If the students generate *RAGS* as a word under *R*, the accompanying question might be What did Cinderella dress in most of the time?

✱ Stretch the use of Alphaboxes across the curriculum to support individual and group work in science, social studies, and math.

Sample

Cinderella

A	B ball	C cinders coachman clock	D dirt dainty
E	F footmen father	G glass slipper	H
I	J	K kind	L
M mean	N no one to help	O	P pumpkin
Q	R rags rats	S slipper stepsisters	T
U unfair	V	W	XYZ

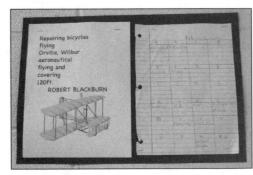

Individually created Alphaboxes support oral retells, reports, and even poetry!

Academic vocabulary is well supported by Alphaboxes as shown in this example from a unit on Native Americans.

Alphaboxes

The book _____

The reader(s) _____

A	B	C	D
E	**F**	**G**	**H**
I	**J**	**K**	**L**
M	**N**	**O**	**P**
Q	**R**	**S**	**T**
U	**V**	**W**	**XYZ**

Two-Word Strategy

The Two-Word Strategy is a nonthreatening way to help students experience inferential reasoning and "beyond the text" thinking. As with all other strategies, it is vital to model and think aloud so students see and hear as you craft Two-Word responses to reading selections. As an example, if you asked students to select two words that reflect their thinking about the price of oil, they might respond with inferences such as:

Two-Word Strategy

Comprehension Strands	Level of Thinking	Action Verbs
Infer	Analyzing	Identify characteristics, main idea
	Generating	Infer, conclude, explain
	Integrating	Connect, make cohesive statements, restructure

Sample

Justification

Word 1	unfair	The high price of oil is impacting every dimension of our economy, driving up prices on food, goods, and travel. It is *unfair* for poor people as they can't even afford to drive their cars.
Word 2	alternatives	We are long overdue in searching for *alternatives* to our dependency on foreign oil.

Note: It is important to word your directions carefully when launching the Two-Word Strategy. If you tell students to generate two words *from the text*, you will get literal-level responses. If you tell them to generate two words that *reflect their thinking* about the text or about a character, they will slip easily into inferences. These examples profile literal-level responses with words from the text.

The two word strategy helps us reflect about our reading.

BOOK TITLE:
Whales Passing

communication   pod

I chose these words because...
all through the book, the pod was communicating with one another about the people while the people communicated

This poster, created during a teacher think-aloud, provides ongoing visual support to students as they use the strategy.

Dinosaurs   Two-Word Strategy   Jonatha 12/19/10

dinosaurs   T-Rex

Dinosaurs are big and tough. They can kill people and weaker dinosaurs.

T-Rex was the biggest dinosaurs in the world. Also it could eat people and weaker dinosaurs to

The Two-Word Strategy was used at Reeds Elementary to help students focus on main ideas.

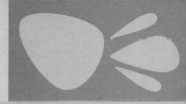

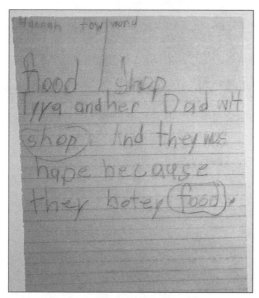

Hannah responds to a Robert Munsch book using the Two-Word Strategy.

As a listening activity:

1. Read a thought-provoking selection to your students (picture book, newspaper article, passage from a resource book, and so on).

2. After reading, ask students to be *silent* and then to write *only two words* (not in a phrase) that reflect their thinking about the passage. At first it may be helpful to provide a half sheet of paper with a box for each focus word. This helps the students understand that the words do not have to be related or in a phrase.

3. After selecting their words, students turn to someone close to them and read their words, tell why they chose them, and explain how they relate to the story and/or their personal lives.

4. At this point, it works well to create a class list of words that were chosen by various individuals. As each word is added to the list and the rationale for selection is shared, a rich tapestry of understandings about the story begins to surface. Students really enjoy hearing the diverse interpretations and benefit from the wealth of vocabulary that appears on the class list.

The Two-Word Strategy causes students to reflect on the entire selection and relate their own world knowledge to the story *without stress.* "only two words?" is a common reaction from students. It sounds easy. It is fun, and it causes deep and intensive reflection!

Note: Another benefit is the wait time that is automatically provided as students write their words. This allows all learners, even those most challenged, to have time to collect their thoughts and be ready to engage in the conversation.

When the Two-Word strategy is linked to writing and retelling, students use richer vocabulary and reach for deeper levels of thought.

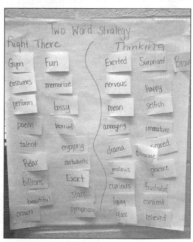

Words generated with the Two-Word Strategy can be easily sorted while comparing words from the text *with words that reflect students'* thinking about the text.

Extension Ideas

✳ Have students select one word that they think is the most helpful in reflecting on the selection then write it on an index card. On the back of the card, ask them to tell why they chose this word and how it relates to the reading. Students then meet in groups to share and compare their words.

✳ Link the Two-Word Strategy to an Alphabox, pages 30–31, and then have students use the words in the Alphabox to generate a retell that is rich in inferential thinking and high-quality vocabulary. The following Alphabox was created by primary students after doing a Two-Word Strategy about *Goldilocks and the Three Bears*.

✳ Students benefit from comparing important words that are within a text with those they can infer about the text. This helps them build a personal definition of the difference between determining importance and inferring while building a strong platform for vocabulary that can use utilized in conversations and in writing.

Sample

Goldilocks and the Three Bears

A	B breaking and entering	C	D
E	F	G	H
I	J jail	K	L locked doors
M	N no manners	O	P pay for repairs problem to parents
Q	R rude girl repair damage	S shocked bears	T trusting
U	V	W	XYZ

The Two-Word Strategy

Name of reader _____

Title of book _____

```
┌─────────────────────────┐    ┌─────────────────────────┐
│                         │    │                         │
│                         │    │                         │
│                         │    │                         │
│                         │    │                         │
│                         │    │                         │
│                         │    │                         │
│                         │    │                         │
│                         │    │                         │
│                         │    │                         │
│                         │    │                         │
└─────────────────────────┘    └─────────────────────────┘
```

Word 1   **Word 2**

I chose these words because _____

_____

_____

_____

_____

_____

_____

Inference Equation

Inferential thinking is often seen as the cornerstone of comprehension (Keene 2008). It is an essential building block of understanding in that we must combine prior knowledge with information gathered from observing, reading, discussing, and so on. When new information is merged with existing knowledge, new understandings develop and comprehension is enhanced.

The Inference Equation provides a visual way to help students see that inference is like a mathematical equation. It requires that things be "added up" or merged to create an inference.

When I am teaching inference, I often make transparencies of interesting photographs then think aloud showing the students how I can use information from the photo plus my prior knowledge to create a new inference. While modeling, I am careful to use the stem "I can infer..." to give the students language with which they can label the cognitive process.

With this photo as our focus, the Inference Equation might guide my think-aloud in the following way:

Inference Equation

Comprehension Strands	Level of Thinking	Action Verbs
Infer	Generating	Infer, conclude
Synthesize	Integrating	Connect, combine

For students to comprehend deeply, they must reach beyond surface-level knowledge to link to prior knowledge and infer.

Example

Background Note: This is my husband with our fishing boat. A freak wave in the bay picked up the boat and dropped it on the beach nearly twenty feet above the waterline. Luckily, no one was hurt.

Information + (clue)	My Prior = Knowledge	I Can Infer...
As I look at the photo, I see the boat is above the waterline.	I know a boat cannot move unless it is in the water or on a trailer.	I can infer that this boat isn't going anywhere until someone can get it in the water or the owner gets a trailer!

Inference Equation

Name _____ Date _____

| Information (clues) | + | my prior knowledge | = | inference. |

Spend time really thinking about inferences. Try to notice times when you infer. If you smell something good coming from the kitchen, can you infer what it is? If you notice your teacher looking unhappy, can you infer what is wrong? Look all around in your life. Notice inferences in your reading. Record your inferences below.

Clues . . . (from real life or from a book)	What I already know . . .	I can infer . . .
Example: There are big, black clouds in the sky.	Dark clouds can mean rain.	I can infer that it is going to rain.

Making Inferences About Characters

Select words that describe characters in a story, a biography, or a historical event.

Name of reader _____ Date _____

Reading selection _____

Character _____

I think this character is _____ because _____

_____

_____

_____

Character _____

I think this character is _____ because _____

_____

_____

_____

Character Descriptions to Consider			
bold	bossy	brave	courageous
cowardly	dangerous	dashing	daring
modest	audacious	fearless	afraid
confused	clever	timid	nervous
shy	tentative	oblivious	sneaky	kind

In the Text/I Can Infer... Charts

As students learn to determine importance, extracting key words and ideas from a text, they quickly find that sometimes the best word or phrase to capture the essence of a passage isn't in the text at all. To facilitate and support the key role of inference in determining importance, summarizing, and synthesizing, I model my thinking aloud about a text using an In the Text/I Can Infer... Chart.

As I move through a text, the objective is to select key words and ideas that capture essential understandings and write them on sticky notes. With each selection, I pause and think aloud, "Was this in the text? Or is this an inference?" I then place a sticky note on the correct side of the chart. After a few sticky notes are placed on the chart, I pause and do a midstream retell, challenging myself to include words and phrases from both sides of the chart. The inclusion of inferences leads to quality generalizations, richer vocabulary, and concise summary statements.

In the Text/I Can Infer...Charts

Comprehension Strands	Level of Thinking	Action Verbs
Infer	Generating	Conclude, explain, infer
Determine importance	Summarizing	
Synthesize	Generating	

This inference strategy captures comprehension that is efferent (in the text), as well as critical/analytical (about the text), and bridges students from rote-level recall to higher-order thinking. With a bit of practice, students quickly learn to employ this strategy in their writer's notebooks, note-taking for social studies and science, and on charts such as the one that follows.

Think-alouds that utilize an In the Text/I Can Infer... chart help students to classify their thinking as they move through the text.

In the Text/I Can Infer . . .

Reader _____ Date _____

The text _____

As you read, select words and phrases that capture important ideas. Be sure to get a balance of items taken directly from the text as well as words and phrases that show your thinking about the text.

In the Text	I Can Infer . . .

Write a summary of the passage and challenge yourself to use as many words and phrases from your chart as you can. When you use items from the I Can Infer . . . side of the chart, underline them and be prepared to share with a partner why you selected those words and phrases.

Understanding a Character and Hot Seat

Understanding a Character

For this retelling structure, I place strips of paper with the names of story characters in a basket and have students pull out a strip to see which character each person will represent.

1. To prepare for a whole-class activity, I divide the number of key characters into the number of students in the class to decide how many individuals need to represent each character. (For example: A story has five characters and I have twenty-five students in class. I will make five strips for each character in the story so that every student in class will be able to draw a strip from the basket. In this case, five students will represent each character.)

2. The students draw their strips from the basket to determine which character they represent. They then return to the text to review and prepare to talk about their character's role in the story.

3. Students meet in "same character" groups to talk about their character's role in the story and create a list of words that best describe their character.

4. The activity moves into a jigsaw format. Groups that have at least one person representing each character are created. These "heterogeneous" groups share about the role of each of their characters in the story, using the text to make points as needed, and explaining their character's behavior in the story.

Note: If this is a small-group activity, skip Step 3 and move directly into the conversation about the characters.

Hot Seat

Hot Seat is an interactive experience that can be used with either literature or content-area studies.

Students are divided into groups with each group becoming an "expert."

Understanding a Character and Hot Seat

Comprehension Strands	Level of Thinking	Action Verbs
Infer	Analyzing	Analyze, examine relationships, identify characteristics
Synthesize	Generating	Conclude, predict, explain, elaborate, infer

* If the topic is literature, then each group could become an expert on a character. In this case they need to be ready to justify that character's behavior in the story. Groups could also become expert on the author's use of characterization, theme, setting, plot, and so forth.

* If the topic is content-area study, expert groups can be formed by dividing the topic into meaningful subtopics such as the food, clothing, and housing of the Iroquois Indians.

It is the responsibility of the group to endure that all members understand the information and are prepared to be questioned.

Hot Seat Rules

One group is asked to form a semicircle facing the front of the class while audience members take turns posing questions. As each question is asked, the expert group puts their heads together and decides on a *team answer*. (An egg timer is a nice way to limit the time they spend deliberating.) The audience member who asked the question then calls on *one* member of the expert group to verbalize the team answer. Since the group has no idea who will be called upon, they must participate fully while the team answer is selected and then ensure that all members are ready to give the answer.

Students really seem to enjoy the security of the group answer and are challenged by the diversity of this experience. Depending on the text, this could focus on simple recall, in-depth character analysis, or a rich discussion of literacy elements. This is a great way to ensure that students of all ability levels learn key information and experience success!

The Character and Me

Invite students to select a character from a story and then compare the character to themselves. In what ways are they alike or different? Do they have similar interests or ways of doing things? If the student had the character's role in the story, would he or she have made an different choices?

A Venn diagram works well for this activity and students find it especially appealing if you have photocopies or digital pictures of the reader and the character and make them available to paste onto the page.

The Character and Me

Comprehension Strands	Level of Thinking	Action Verbs
Determine Importance	Organizing	Compare, contrast
Connect	Analyzing	Differentiate, identify characteristics

Examples

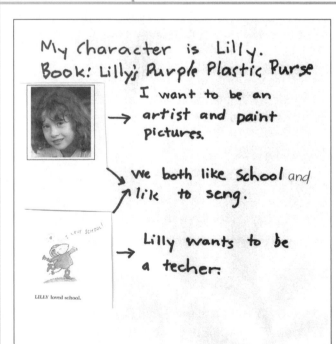

My character is Lilly.
Book: Lilly's Purple Plastic Purse

→ I want to be an artist and paint pictures.

↘ We both like school and
↗ lik to seng.

→ Lilly wants to be a techer.

LILLY loved school.

Name of Character: The author never gives him a name.
Name of Book: Drummer Boy by Ann Turner
Name of Reader: Robert

Describe the Character:
Brave, Excited, Angry

The drummer boy starts out __brave__ and __excited__ to be part of the war but he realizes how terrible it is and gets __angry__. He is furious at Abraham Lincoln. The drummer boy had a lot of courage but he was also very unhappy. He left his family for the wrong reasons and should have stayed with his parents.

In what ways are you alike? *I get excited about things too and sometimes wish I had taken more time to think before I make decisions. We both care about our family. I would miss my parents if I had to go away like he did. I would like to learn to play the drums too but just for the music, not for a war.*

Describe Yourself:
Busy, a reader, soccer player

I have a very __busy__ life as __a soccer player__ and lots of activities with my family. I like to __read__ many different kinds of books. As I think about my life compared to the drummer boy, I realize that war causes you to make decisions you might not make otherwise.

The Character and Me

Name of character _____

Name of book _____

Name of reader _____

Describe yourself:

_____ , _____ , _____

photo of child

In what ways are you alike? ⟶

photocopy image of character

Describe the character:

_____ , _____ , _____

V.I.P. ("Very Important Points")

Have students cut sticky notes so that there are slim strips of paper extending out from the sticky edge.

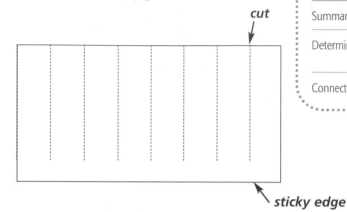

As students read, they can then tear off these pieces of fringe to mark points in the text that they feel are significant. These may be points of interest, points of confusion, or points where the student felt a personal connection.

As a postreading activity, students can compare the points they marked and tell why they chose to mark each one. There are no prefabricated questions. Readers simply talk to each other about what they read, using the self-sticking notes as points of reference. It is critical that these VIPs (Very Important Points) be justified in the conversation. As students share their VIPs, they need to make statements such as "I chose to mark this point *because . . .*"

Ideally, the teacher serves as a group member sharing personal VIPs and the rationale for choosing each one.

To support emergent readers in learning this strategy, I find it helpful to start with predictable books. I read to them while they follow along for a page or two. We then talk about the pictures and the author's message. Each child is asked to place one VIP on either a part of a picture or a point in the text and then tell why that spot is important. After several experiences, emergent readers find this is a very supportive retelling structure, and they are eager to share VIP observations.

As students gain sophistication with this strategy, they can use it for longer segments of text knowing that the VIPs will help them to reflect and summarize. With some students, I

V.I.P. ("Very Important Points")

Comprehension Strands	Level of Thinking	Action Verbs
Summarize	Knowing	Identify, store information
Determine Importance	Analyzing	Examine, main idea, determine importance
Connect	Evaluating	Judge evaluate, rate

find they enjoy working with one paragraph or one page at a time and then building into longer segments of text.

Evaluative thinking and oral interactions can also be stimulated when students are asked to work in pairs and determine the four or five most important issues in a story or a unit of study. To accomplish this, partners must first reflect on all their VIPs, evaluate the importance of each piece of information, and then collaboratively rank them. Older students studying the American Civil War had a fascinating discussion when the partners each presented and attempted to justify their rankings of the war's five most important events. Primary students eagerly talked well into recess time after using this process with *The Velveteen Rabbit.*

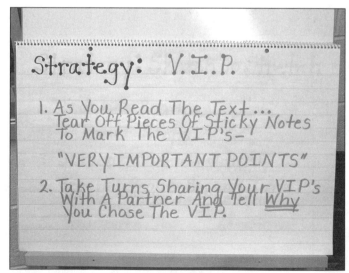

Posters and charts remind students of the steps in using the VIP Strategy.

Middle school students use the VIP Strategy to identify important ideas.

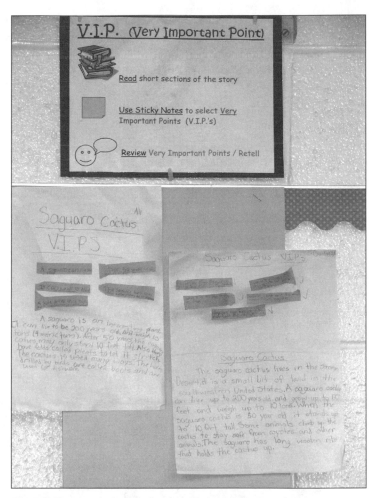

The VIP Strategy helps students write better summaries.

Identifying VIPs in novels and nonfiction texts helps prevent short-term memory overload and supports content retention.

When students learn to ask questions of themselves and their conversation partners, they remember more and become more fully engaged with the text selection. The personal questions readers generate about a text stimulate connections, represent inferences, activate prior knowledge, and help them to clarify understanding.

As you guide students in generating questions, remember to assist them in generating questions and responses that are aesthetic, efferent, and critical/analytical. These levels of questioning support broad ranges of understanding, stimulate language use, and are powerful supports to partner conversations.

Stimulating Discussion Through Questions

Comprehension Strands	Level of Thinking	Action Verbs
Question	Knowing	Formulate questions
Infer	Generating	Produce new understandings
Connect	Evaluating	Judge, evaluate, rate

A caution: It is not necessary to begin conversations with efferent questions. Sometimes the best conversations begin with aesthetic responses that engage emotion and qualitative thinking.
(P. David Pearson 2008)

The teacher scaffolds and stimulates students to reach deeper with questions that expand understanding.

Students who expect to question a text read more thoughtfully and engage in critical thinking.

Types of Questions

Aesthetic: **Expressive responses that invite learners to share their thinking.**

What was your favorite part? Why?

Which character did you find most intriguing? Why?

If you were the author, which part of the story would bring you the most pride?

Are there any parts of this selection that you would change?

At which points were you best able to visualize or "see" the action?

What did the author do that helped you connect to this selection?

Efferent: **Unpacking the facts of the text.**

Who, what, when, where?

In what order?

Which character was central to the story?

Describe the climax.

From which point of view is this selection written?

If we were to identify the most important ideas, what would they be?

Compare the events in this story with the events in _____.

Critical/analytical: **Students interrogate the text, the author, the issue, and the purpose.**

What important issues were addressed in this selection? Why are these important?

What does the author want you to believe or understand? What is the author's point of view?

How might we verify the accuracy of this selection?

If we were to evaluate this selection, what criteria might we consider?

Quality Questions

Partner #1 _____ Partner #2 _____ Date _____

With a partner, think of two questions about the text that would *stimulate* conversation.

#1 _____

_____

_____

_____

#2 _____

_____

_____

_____

Meet with another partner pair. Share your questions with each other.

Which questions would you agree are most likely to stimulate deep conversations on this topic?

_____

_____

_____

Bring your questions to the whole group and be ready to discuss your reading.

"I Wonder..."

Before Reading

(Look at the cover of the book and think of ways to complete this stem.)

I Wonder _____

I Wonder _____

I Wonder _____

During Reading

(Stop at least twice during reading to generate more "I Wonder" statements.)

I Wonder _____

I Wonder _____

I Wonder _____

After Reading

(Provide time to reflect on the text and then consider additional "I Wonder" statements that might reflect the content and/or the author's craft.)

I Wonder _____

I Wonder _____

I Wonder _____

Book Commercials

Commercials and advertisements are a part of nearly every American child's life and can provide the foundation for exciting reflections on favorite stories and units of study.

Samples

Are you tired of being hungry? Wondering where your next meal will come from and which day of the week you might find it? At 8:00 p.m. every Monday on Channel 8 you can join *The Very Hungry Caterpillar* for your most challenging food solutions!

Are you aware that a young boy named Brian recently crash-landed a plane in the wilderness of Canada **ALL BY HIMSELF**? He survived the crash, then lived on berries and lived through incredible acts of nature. To learn more about his incredible adventure, check out the fiction section of the library under *Hatchet* by Gary Paulsen.

Did you know that there is a woman who loves to wash muddy animals? She washes pigs and cows and ducks. She tries to keep them clean—but they keep running back into the mud. Check out *Mrs. Wish-Washy* to find out what happens!

Write your own!

Partner book commercials engage all learners and support differentiation.

Newscasters must report summaries in clear, concise terms that keep a listener engaged.

Book Commercial Form

Name of copywriter for this ad _____ Date _____

Media to be used: radio ad, television ad, magazine ad, newspaper ad, other

The book to be advertised _____

Important characters _____

Important points_____

Art for the ad:

My opening question: _____

_____

Details for the middle: _____

_____

An ending that will sell this book: _____

_____

_____

_____

Memorable Moments

Reader _____

Before I read the story, I anticipated that a memorable moment would be _____

_____

_____

As I finished the story, I realized the most memorable moment was _____

_____

_____

Another moment that was worthy of attention was _____

_____

_____

I have selected the following quote as an example of how the author created the memorable moment: Page number _____

_____

_____

_____

_____

_____

_____

Drawing Conclusions

When readers draw conclusions from their reading, it is much easier to make generalizations and determine important ideas.

Reader _____ Text _____ Topic _____ Date _____

Facts from my reading: _____

_____

_____

_____

_____

Conclusions I can draw include: _____

_____

_____

_____

_____

I believe the very most important ideas are: _____

_____

_____

_____

Maybe

rovide the students with a statement that is controversial. Their task is to come up with a list of reasons (pro and con) for why this statement may or may not be true.

Maybe

Comprehension Strands	Level of Thinking	Action Verbs
Infer	Generating	Conclude, explain, infer
Synthesize	Integrating	Connect and combine, generalize
	Organizing	Compare, contrast

Example #1

Cinderella's fairy godmother should have given her more time to enjoy her beautiful dress and fancy carriage.

Agree:

She spent too long in rags.

Disagree:

The story would have turned out very differently if she hadn't had to run from the ball.

Example #2

Little Red Riding Hood's mother shouldn't have sent her to grandmother's house by herself.

Agree:

It is dangerous for young children to walk alone through a forest.

Disagree:

Children need to learn to be independent. If she knows the way and it is usually safe, she should be able to go visit her grandmother.

The Maybe Strategy engages students in comparing and contrasting ideas, drawing conclusions, and learning to justify their thinking with evidence from the text.

Revisit, Reflect, Retell ✳ UPDATED EDITION

Maybe

Controversial statement about a book, a character, or a current event.

Agree   Disagree

_____   _____

_____   _____

_____   _____

_____   _____

_____   _____

_____   _____

_____   _____

_____   _____

Group members _____

_____

_____

Analyzing Poetry

Reader _____ Date _____

While reading and discussing poetry today, I thought:

The most interesting theme was _____.

My favorite poem was _____

_____ because _____.

_____

I was able to get the best visualization when I read _____

_____. The author helped my visualization by

_____

_____

_____.

The big ideas were easier to identify when I remembered to _____

_____

_____.

If I were to write a poem, I would want to be sure to _____

_____

_____

_____.

Get Real

Good story writers often want their characters to have traits that resemble people in the real world. Your job is to select a character from your story and consider how realistic that character may be. Review your story and select quotes that show whether the character is realistic.

Book _____ Character _____

Quote #1: _____

_____

_____

I selected this quote because _____

_____

_____

Quote #2: _____

_____

_____

I selected this quote because _____

_____

_____

Quote #3: _____

_____

_____

I selected this quote because _____

_____

_____

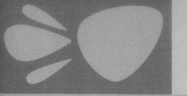

Have a Book Party

Model a book talk designed to generate interest and enthusiasm for reading a particular title. Then, plan a book party to celebrate meaningful book sharing. A Book Party can occur within a classroom, as an activity between two classrooms, or as a parent involvement activity.

Have a Book Party		
Comprehension Strands	**Level of Thinking**	**Action Verbs**
Synthesize	Evaluating	Judge, rate, assess, summarize
	Integrating	

* Let the students know in advance that there will be a book sharing opportunity. It makes it seem more special if the date and time are posted and an invitation is created.

* Everyone needs to do a lot of reading to consider a range of books before selecting the special one that is shared at the Book Party. They might choose a text because they have read it fully. They also could select one they are in the process of reading or are hoping to read soon.

* Participants rehearse their book talks to ensure that they do not take more than two minutes and that the book talk creates interest in the listeners.

* At the Book Party, participants sit in circles or at tables. It is very important to sit so everyone makes eye contact.

* My students really enjoy combining the book talks with refreshments to create a "party" atmosphere. You might consider serving hot chocolate with peppermint sticks for stirring, or another favorite treat.

Book Party Variations

* Cross-age gatherings of students. Think broadly here: it even works to bring Head Start children and elementary Title 1 students together!

* Celebrating student-authored books.

* Author studies. Each group selects an author whose books they choose.

* Theme studies. Each group selects a genre or a theme for their book selections.

* Magazine party.

* A comedy party with "comic" moments for cartoons and comic books.

* Joke and riddle party.

* Poetry party.

Partnership Observations

Partners: _____

Date	Book Being Read and Discussed	Partners are actively listening	Both partners take responsibility for talk	Partners support/assist each other	Conversations include:	Forming opinions	Asking questions	Use of evidence from text	Connections T-T,T-W,T-S	Inferences	Comparisons	Linking/extending ideas

Talking About Stories

Student Name _____

Book _____

1. I read the story carefully.

2. I used the pictures to help me remember the important parts of the story.

3. I talked about the story with my partners.

4. I listened to my partners.

5. I asked questions.

6. I learned _____

_____

7. My favorite part was _____

_____

Reflection Group: Self-Assessment

Name _____ Date _____

Today I participated: ☐ Too much   ☐ Too little   ☐ Just the right amount

My most important contribution to the discussion was _____

_____

Our group is getting better at _____

_____

We still need to work on _____

_____

Rating Scale

    5 great job
    4 pretty good
    3 I could do better
    2 I need to make a plan for improving

My Score

_____   1. I read the selection thoughtfully.
_____   2. I marked key points in the text with sticky notes.
_____   3. I prepared by thinking about what I would say in the group.
_____   4. I stayed on the topic.
_____   5. I compared the story to my life and to other books I have read.
_____   6. I thought about critical story elements.
_____   7. I asked questions when I didn't understand.
_____   8. I had eye contact with members of my group.
_____   9. I encouraged others to speak.
_____ 10. I was a good listener.

_____   **My total for today**

I am getting better at _____

_____

Literature Circle Scoring Guide

This scoring guide is meant to stimulate an oral interaction that asks group members to consider these questions and respond to each about how their group functioned. The goal is to use this reflection as a lead-in to goal-setting as groups strive to improve the quality of their teamwork and conversations.

Today in our group...

	(5) Everyone was awesome					(0) It was a hard day
Everyone contributed.	5	4	3	2	1	0
We stayed on task.	5	4	3	2	1	0
We worked as a team.	5	4	3	2	1	0
We kept eye contact.	5	4	3	2	1	0
We were active listeners.	5	4	3	2	1	0
There was a lot of piggybacking in our conversation.	5	4	3	2	1	0
We justified our opinions with examples from the book.	5	4	3	2	1	0

Our goal for the next time is to improve _____

_____

_____

_____

Group Discussion Rating

Name _____ Date _____

Book _____

My Group

We knew what to do.	1 2 3 4 5	We were confused.
Everyone contributed.	1 2 3 4 5	Some people contributed.
We stayed on task.	1 2 3 4 5	We slipped off topic.
We worked together.	1 2 3 4 5	We worked independently.
We made team decisions.	1 2 3 4 5	Group decisions were difficult.

Myself

I contributed ideas.	1 2 3 4 5	I didn't say much.
I was an active listener.	1 2 3 4 5	I had a hard time listening.
I encouraged the other team members.	1 2 3 4 5	I forgot to do this.
I tried to be open to new ideas.	1 2 3 4 5	I wanted things to go my way.
I kept eye contact with the person speaking.	1 2 3 4 5	I forgot to do this.
I learned a lot today.	1 2 3 4 5	I didn't learn much today.
I am proud of my contribution today.	1 2 3 4 5	I need to try harder.

Overall Rating

We had a great discussion.	1 2 3 4 5	We need to do better next time.

Teacher Observation: Interactions with Books

Student Name _____ Date _____

	Usually	**Sometimes**	**Rarely**
1. Engages with books independently.	☐	☐	☐
2. Chooses to read during free time.	☐	☐	☐
3. Can express thoughts about a text with an adult.	☐	☐	☐
4. Can express thoughts about a text with peers.	☐	☐	☐
5. Can justify opinions about a story.	☐	☐	☐
6. Draws on personal experiences when talking about stories.	☐	☐	☐
7. Can be specific when telling what is or is not liked about a book.	☐	☐	☐
8. Can listen to others express their thoughts.	☐	☐	☐
9. Uses references to text structure such as plot, problem, and solution.	☐	☐	☐
10. Uses references to stylistic elements such as figurative language, mood, and so on.	☐	☐	☐

Group Discussion Log

Book being discussed _____ Author _____

Date _____ Teacher _____

Key: ✓ well done
    – needs support

Names of participants	#1	#2	#3	#4
Read and prepared for conversation.	☐	☐	☐	☐
Noted points in text to include in discussion.	☐	☐	☐	☐
Contributed to the dialogue.	☐	☐	☐	☐
Asked relevant, meaningful questions.	☐	☐	☐	☐
Used the text to support and clarify points.	☐	☐	☐	☐
Encouraged others to talk.	☐	☐	☐	☐
Made inferences beyond the text.	☐	☐	☐	☐
Referred to story elements such as plot, setting, characterization, conflict, and resolution.	☐	☐	☐	☐
Referred to the author's use of literary elements such as mood, theme, tension, and so on.	☐	☐	☐	☐

Talking About Books at Home

Dear Parent,

One of the best things we can do to assist our children with reading is to engage them in talking about the books they read. Talking stimulates language development and helps children improve their comprehension.

As you get ready to share a book with your child, you might ask your child to talk about the cover, the title, and a few of the pictures in the book. This "before-reading" conversation will help your child to build the expectation that stories make sense. This is also a good time to help your child connect personal experiences to the reading. If there is a picture showing a picnic, for example, this would be a perfect time to talk with your child about a picnic you enjoyed together.

You can also invite your child into conversation during the reading by stopping now and then to ask, "What might happen next?"

As you know, children love to share their opinions. After reading, you might get your child started with questions such as:

* What did you notice?

* What did you like?

* How did it make you feel?

* Did this remind you of any experiences you have had?

* What parts of the story were your favorites?

Just choose one or two questions so that if feels like a conversation instead of a test. Happy reading!

Sincerely,

Your child's teacher

Strategy Celebration

Dear Parent(s),

Your child has learned a wide range of strategies to support reading comprehension. Please plan to take time tonight to celebrate the _____ Strategy

(name of strategy)

with your child. Your child is prepared to teach you the strategy and be your partner in reading and learning together.

The form below will provide a place for you to describe your experience. Please sign this form and return it to school so your child can celebrate his or her experience with the rest of the class.

My child taught us the _____ Strategy.

We practiced it in _____.

(name of book or reading selection)

We learned _____

_____

_____

_____.

We liked this strategy because _____

_____

_____.

Signed _____   _____

(Parent)   (Child)

Linking At-Home Reading to Class
Strategy Lessons: Inference

Date _____ **Book Title** _____

Inferences I made while reading at home:

1._____

2._____

3._____

4._____

Parent signature_____

Inference based on page _____.

_____

_____

_____

_____

Date _____ **Book Title** _____

Inferences I made while reading at home:

1._____

2._____

3._____

4._____

Parent signature_____

Inference based on page _____.

_____

_____

_____

_____

Date _____ **Book Title** _____

Inferences I made while reading at home:

1._____

2._____

3._____

4._____

Parent signature_____

Inference based on page _____.

_____

_____

_____

_____

Retelling Strategy	Comprehension Strands	Classification of Thinking	Page
Preparing for a Retell	Summarize	Integrating	77
	Determine importance	Analyzing	
		Evaluating	
Retelling Checklist for Fiction	Summarize	Integrating	78
	Determine importance	Analyzing	
Illustrating the Story	Use sensory imaging	Organizing	79
	Summarize	Integrating	
Three-Circle Map	Summarize	Integrating	80
	Use sensory imaging	Analyzing	
What Is Important?	Determine importance	Evaluating	82
Partner Retelling	Determine importance	Evaluating	84
	Summarize	Knowing	
Novel Reflections	Determine importance	Analyzing	87
		Integrating	
Team Retelling	Summarize	Organizing	88
Spin a Story	Summarize	Organizing	91
Paper Bag Theatre, Story Bag, Storytelling at the Overhead, and Storytelling Apron and Storytelling Vest	Use sensory imaging	Organizing	94
Hand Print Retells and Storytelling Glove	Summarize	Organizing	96
		Generating	
Compare and Contrast	Synthesize	Organizing	97
		Evaluating	
Retells on Tape	Summarize	Integrating	98
	Synthesize	Evaluating	
Support Retell and Summary with Dramatic Interpretation	Use sensory imaging	Organizing	98
	Synthesize	Evaluating	
Spicing It Up with Line Drawings	Use sensory imaging	Organizing	98
Cumulative Retells	Summarize	Organizing	99

Oral Retelling

3

The best retells spring from high-quality text, stimulating students to think deeply and retell or summarize in concise terms.

Retelling is a reflection tool that requires readers to organize information they've gleaned from the text in order to provide a personalized summary. Students engaging in retells must review all they know about a text; select key points that reflect main ideas; consider key events, problem, solution, characters, and setting, then weave the information into a meaningful communication. Retelling has been found to significantly improve comprehension and sense of story structure while enhancing oral language proficiency (Hoyt 2006).

The following sequence provides a frame for retelling in the classroom:

- Tell the students *why* retelling is important. They need to know how a retell helps them as readers and as effective communicators. It is helpful to demonstrate a retell by summarizing a popular movie or describing a

Model retells so students clearly understand the goal.

favorite vacation to show the students how retelling fits into our lives both in and outside of school. Students can tell about family outings, about playing with their pets, or about favorite activities such as bicycling. Retelling life events is a natural part of our lives.

- Demonstrate retells that encompass key literary elements as part of shared reading or read-aloud experiences. As in all learning, thinking aloud about how you reviewed the text and decided what to say helps students to understand the cognitive process they will need to implement. At this introductory stage, it is helpful to have a visual example you can point to as you move through the components of the retell, such as the list on page 72. Be explicit as you model so that students understand a retell doesn't include *everything*. It focuses on important ideas in an informational text and on the plot in a fiction selection.

Scaffold quality retells with graphic organizers and retelling props.

- Depending on the age of the students, you might want to start with a brief passage and then begin demonstrating with longer, more complex texts. It is also helpful during this demonstration stage to retell expository as well as narrative selections. While I am in this demonstration stage, I often ask the students to evaluate my retell to see if I omitted any important parts. By observing models of self-evaluation as well as the retelling process, students develop a stronger understanding of the steps they will need to follow when working independently.

- Self-evaluate your retells in front of the students, thinking aloud about the elements you included and your ability to make it interesting.

Caution: It is very important to monitor authenticity of retelling experiences. If children are asked to retell a story or a life event to the same individual who listened to them read or who shared the experience, the child may perceive the interaction as a test.

- While demonstrating how to do a retell it is helpful to provide students with suggestions on how to be a good listener. Again, a visual may help students become more effective listeners:

Good Listeners...

Have eye contact with the storyteller

Listen carefully

Think about parts of the retell without talking out loud

Are ready to say something positive about the retell

Save questions for the end

- Guide students as they practice. During the initial practice stage most students enjoy working in partners or groups with others who have read the same text. The activities on the following pages provide a wide range of options for this stage. It is also very helpful if students have visual supports when they are attempting their first retells.

Students need to know that their retells have an authentic purpose.

Authentic audience is essential as students learn that retells aren't just a "test."

- Another step is to work with the students to utilize voice changes, develop shifts in pacing, and add a sense of drama to the "telling" of a story. This has proven very meaningful to many students and carries over to public speaking and expressive oral reading.

Narrative Retelling

Title and Author

Main Idea: The plot

Key Characters

The Setting

The Problem

Key Events

The Resolution

- Help students personalize retelling as a private learning strategy. Good readers continually reflect as they read, sifting through events and understandings. Readers need to understand that retelling is something you can do privately to enhance your own understanding and memory. When internalized and applied consciously, retelling becomes a tool for lifelong learning.

  To facilitate this internalization, I often stop students during independent reading time, or during a content area such as science or math, and suggest that they take a moment to reflect and do a silent retell in their head. The goal is to transfer ownership of the process to the learner.

Power Up Retells with Transition Words and Connectives

Transition words and connectives can serve as a powerful stimulus for language expansion in retells and summaries. With support from transition words, students move more easily through a sequence of events and provide more elaboration of content.

I create posters of helpful transition words and keep them in a visible place to support learners during oral retells. I find that when students are coached to use transition words and connectives in their oral communication, these important words begin appearing in their writing as well.

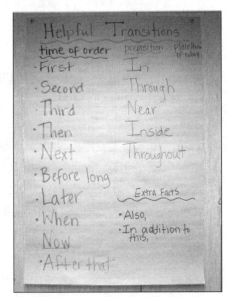

Transition words solidify sequence and add sophistication to retells.

Transition Words

PURPOSE	EXAMPLE OF TRANSITION WORDS
Time/sequence (the order in which something happens)	first, second, third, before, during, after, today, tomorrow, yesterday, until, next, then, as soon as, finally, afterward, earlier, meanwhile, now, since, soon, then
Show place	adjacent to, here, on the opposite side, beyond, nearby, opposite to
Compare/Contrast (show differences)	however, but, although, on the other hand, similarly, even though, still, though, yet, also, likewise, similarly
Conclude, summarize, or emphasize a point (the end of the writing is coming)	finally, in conclusion, therefore, in other words
Add information	first, also, and, besides, in addition, for example, next, finally
Example or illustration	specifically, for example, in fact, of course, to illustrate, for instance

Preparing for a Retell

1. Read a really good story.

2. List or draw the most important events from the story.

3. Read the story again to be sure that you have gotten the most important ideas.

4. Plan for any props that will make your retell interesting to an audience.

5. Practice

   * inside your head
   * to a partner
   * in front of a mirror
   * by talking into a tape recorder

Be sure to remember:

* Characters
* Setting
* Events
* Your Opinion!

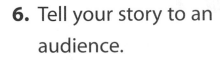

6. Tell your story to an audience.

Retelling Checklist for Fiction

☐ Choose a story you like a lot.

☐ Read it.

☐ Read it again.

☐ Think about the story.

☐ Plan the performance to include information about:

    ✳ characters

    ✳ main character's problem

    ✳ most important events that led to solving the problem

    ✳ the climax

    ✳ the resolution

☐ Speak clearly and loudly enough for all to hear.

☐ Make eye contact with the audience.

☐ Be dramatic!

Illustrating the Story

Have the reader illustrate the beginning, middle, and end of a story, then use the pictures to support a retell. The retelling checklist at the bottom can be either folded back or torn off and saved as an assessment of progress.

Reader _____ Date _____ Book _____

The Beginning   **The Middle**   **The End**

During the oral retell of the story, this reader included:

	Great job!	Almost there	Oops
All main characters	☐	☐	☐
Secondary characters	☐	☐	☐
The setting	☐	☐	☐
The beginning	☐	☐	☐
The middle	☐	☐	☐
The end	☐	☐	☐
The problem	☐	☐	☐
The events were in the correct order	☐	☐	☐
The solution	☐	☐	☐
The author's message	☐	☐	☐

Higher-level response
(opinion, connection, visualization, other): _____

Notes about the retell/implications for instruction: _____

Three-Circle Map

Have students draw and/or write in each circle to show what they remember about key elements of the story, then talk to others about their reflections.

If you ask students to complete the beginning and ending circles first, they anchor their thinking and can then focus on "What was this mostly about" for the middle circle.

Note: this organizer is also a helpful planning device when students are initiating an original piece of writing.

Three-Circle Map

Comprehension Strands	Level of Thinking	Action Vocabulary
Summarize	Integrating	Summarize information into cohesive statement
Use sensory imaging	Analyzing	Outline, diagram

Example

Title: Clifrd lrns to rede

Beginning

Ending

Middle

School

Problem _____
_____
Solution _____
_____

Theme/Plot _____
_____
_____
_____

FIGURE 3–1 *Clifford learns to read.*

Three-Circle Map

Name of reader: _____

The story: _____

_____

Problem: _____

_____

The solution: _____

_____

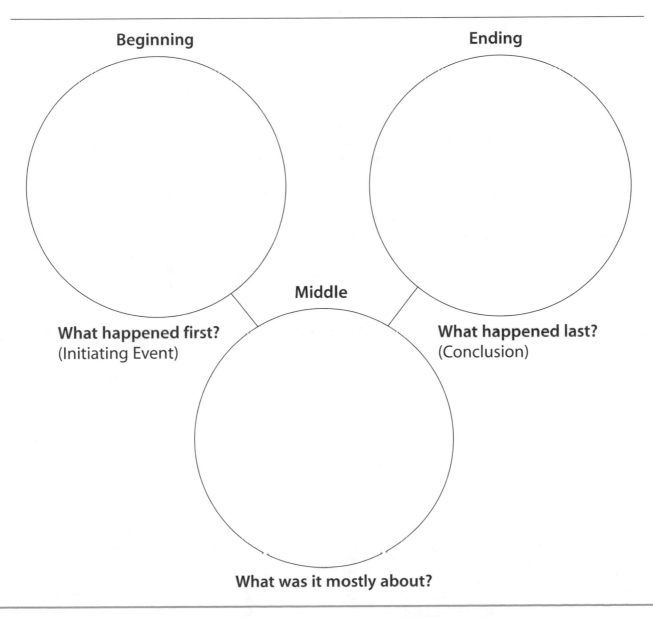

Beginning

Ending

Middle

What happened first?
(Initiating Event)

What happened last?
(Conclusion)

What was it mostly about?

What Is Important?

The importance of this organizer is not the form itself, but rather the thinking and the conversations it can generate. The goal is to help students understand that all events and characters are not of equal importance in a story. As they begin to evaluate comparative levels of importance, nuances of understanding begin to emerge. The important question at all levels is "Why do you think so?"

In working with emergent readers and writers, I might offer to be their secretary and support their discussion while I draw and write their ideas. As children become more proficient both with writing and with using this organizer, it may turn into shared writing, interactive writing with a group, or an independent activity.

What Is Important?		
Comprehension Strands	**Level of Thinking**	**Action Vocabulary**
Determine importance	Evaluating	Judge, rate, evaluate

Directions

✳ Have students reflect on key story elements or facts from a text and list the four believed to be the most critical.

✳ Rank the elements with #1 being least important to the story.

✳ List words under each selected element that describe that element *and/or* provide justification for the ranking.

What Is Important?

The Book _____ Date _____

The Reader _____

Focus on: ( ) Characters   ( ) Events

| **Least Important** | **Moderately Important** | | **Most Important** |
| 1 | 2 | 3 | 4 |

Describing words to justify ranking.

_____   _____   _____   _____

_____   _____   _____   _____

_____   _____   _____   _____

_____   _____   _____   _____

_____   _____   _____   _____

Talk about your rankings.

_____

_____

_____

_____

_____

_____

Partner Retelling

While this experience can be adapted easily to many formats, the following steps might be considered for a whole-class response to a read-aloud story:

1. After reading a story to the students, explain that they will be working on retelling the story. It is helpful to identify the key points for the retelling (e.g., most important events, elements of story structure, and so on).

2. Divide the class in half so there is a storyteller group and a listening group.

3. The storytellers work in teams to reread the selection and remind each other of the focus points for this retell. The listeners also reread and reflect on what they agree to be the most important retell elements of this story.

Partner Retelling

Comprehension Strands	Level of Thinking	Action Vocabulary
Determine importance	Evaluating	Assess, rate, judge, confirm
Summarize	Knowing	List, name, identify

4. The students then are matched with partners, a storyteller and a listener. While the teller talks, the listener records the elements of the story that are provided without assistance. When the storyteller is finished, it is the job of the listener to give clues about any remaining items that have not been checked off on the list.

After the students have experience with this format, it adapts easily to smaller groups of students and a wide range of texts.

Partner retells engage all learners in careful reflection while providing powerful opportunities for teacher assessment.

Partner Retelling Checklist

Name of Partner _____ Name of Listener _____

Date _____ Book _____

Draw a circle around one thing your partner did *very* well today. Put a check mark next to one suggestion for improvement and tell your partner WHY.

The main idea

The characters

The setting

The most important events

The problem

The solution

Partner Retelling

Partner Retelling Activity for (story name) _____

Storyteller (name of student) _____

Listener (name of student) _____

Focus points: (Most important events, problem/solution, characters, setting)	Retold without help	Clues given
_____	☐	☐
_____	☐	☐
_____	☐	☐
_____	☐	☐
_____	☐	☐
_____	☐	☐
_____	☐	☐
_____	☐	☐
_____	☐	☐
_____	☐	☐

Novel Reflections

Draw or write three points for each chapter.

Example: ✳ problem/solution/setting ✳ literary devices ✳ mood
✳ 3 key events ✳ points of tension ✳ shifts in character traits

Title _____ Reader _____

Chapter _____	**Chapter _____**

Team Retelling

Teams of three or four students share responsibility for retelling pertinent aspects of the story structure. The retelling focus is selected by the teacher in response to the needs of a group or as support for elements of text structure currently being studied. Groups might be arranged so that one team looks at problem, solution, and resolution while another team looks at literary devices such as tension, mood, and setting. It also works well to compare these structural elements across several texts.

After reflecting and talking, teams take turns retelling their stories with emphasis on the targeted elements of story design. If the teams have read different selections, the retelling becomes an authentic commercial for the focus stories, hopefully enticing listeners to engage with those same texts. If they have read the same selections, lively discussions about different interpretations can serve to deepen understanding.

I find that it is helpful to provide visuals for these activities. If each team has a set of cards identifying the elements of story structure or the literacy devices being shared during their retelling, both listeners and tellers seem to develop deeper understandings.

Variations include:

✱ It is sometimes fun to add an element of surprise for a group. Individual story structure cards are placed facedown in front of a group and thoroughly shuffled. Group members then draw from the collection of cards to see which story element each will be responsible for telling.

✱ The listeners have a set of individual story structure cards. As the tellers are speaking, the listeners withdraw elements that are being described from the collection of cards. (Example: A storyteller explains the use

Team Retelling		
Comprehension Strands	**Level of Thinking**	**Action Vocabulary**
Summarize	Organizing	Sequence, group

of description and imagery in *Sylvester and the Magic Pebble* by William Steig and the listener removes the card for "Imagery" from the literary devices card collection.) After the telling, the listener(s) can show the storyteller(s) which elements they were especially aware of during the retell.

✱ The cards can also be used to make the organization of the retell more apparent to the listeners. The storytellers might hold up the cards reflecting their focus points before beginning to tell their story and open with statements such as, "Today we are going to retell the story of _____. As we tell our story, please be watching for information about [problem, solution, and theme]." This helps the listeners by giving them a focus for listening, and it helps the storytellers to stay focused on their topic.

Collaborative retells can be organized around story elements such as characters, setting, problem/solution, events, or literary elements.

Team Retelling

Card Set #1: Elements of Story Structure

Plot	**Theme**
Problem	**Solution**
Main Idea	**Setting**
Primary Characters	**Secondary Characters**
Setting	**Key versus Secondary Events**
Point of View	**Climax**

Team Retelling

Card Set #2: Literary Devices

Analogy	Alliteration
Caricature	Atmosphere
Foreshadowing	Flashback-Forward
Mood	Imagery
Simile	Inference
Stereotype	Influence of Pictures
Symbolism	Irony
Tension	Metaphor
Parody	Personification
Poetic Language	Satire

Spin a Story

Team members take turns spinning an arrow that is attached to a tagboard playing surface. Each time their spinner lands on a category, players need to tell something relevant to that dimension of the story. For example, if a student spins and lands on Events, the student would tell about one event. The board is then passed to the next player. That player spins and lands on Characters and then tells something about a character or character development, and so on.

The categories on the playing surface should reflect current teaching points for story structure or areas in which these particular students need additional support.

Spin a Story

Comprehension Strands	Level of Thinking	Action Vocabulary
Summarize	Organizing	Sequence, group

Spinner 1

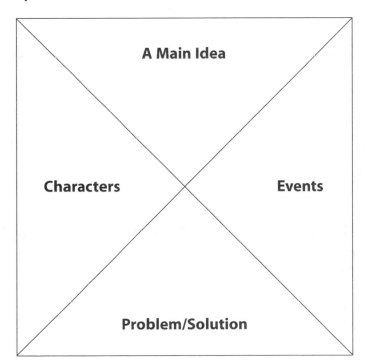

A Main Idea

Characters   Events

Problem/Solution

Spinner 2

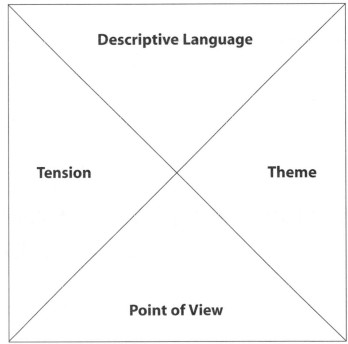

Descriptive Language

Tension   Theme

Point of View

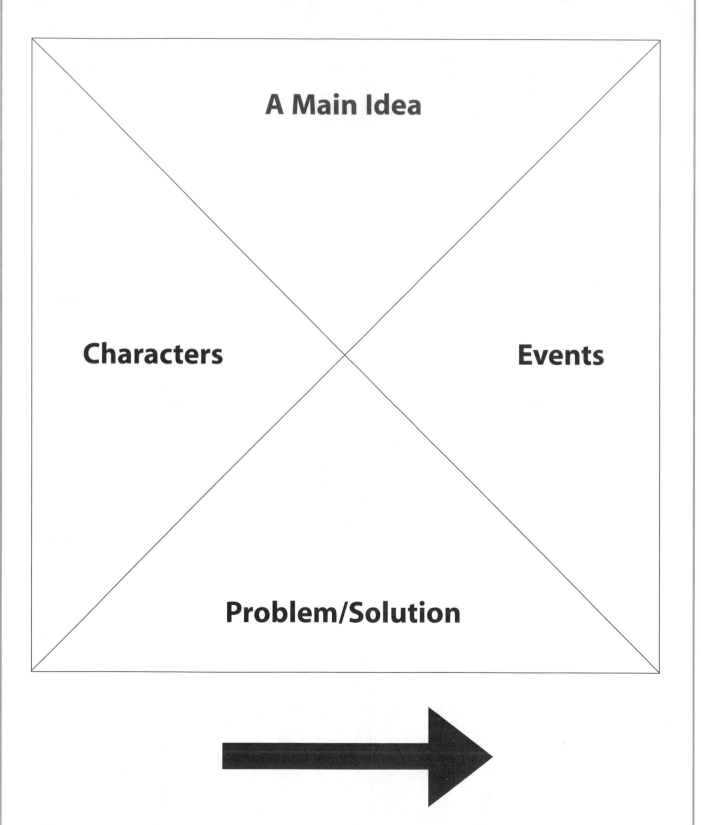

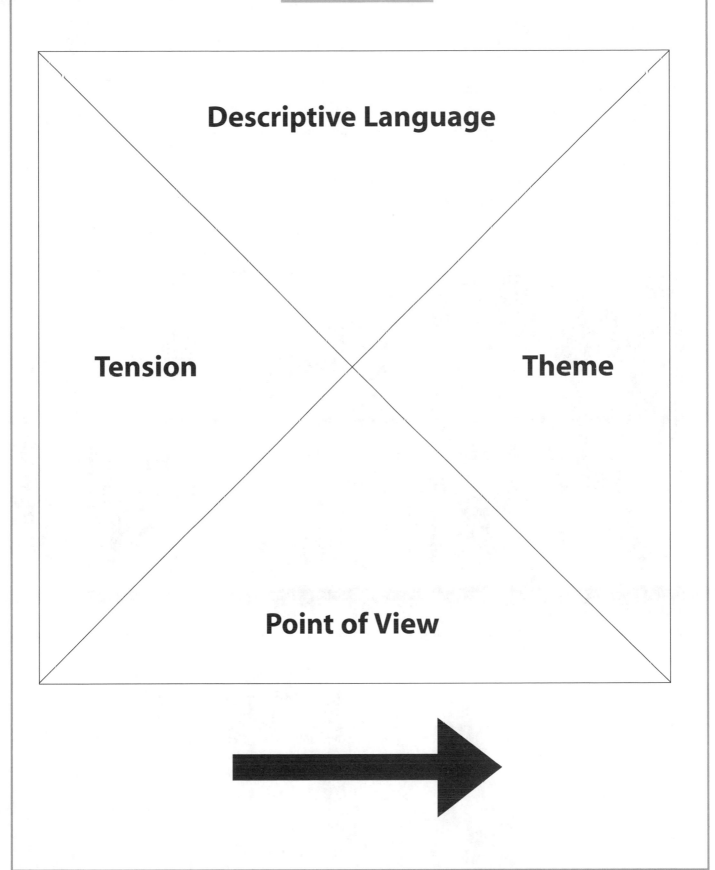

Descriptive Language

Tension

Theme

Point of View

Storytelling with Props

Paper Bag Theatre

Students illustrate a key setting from a story on the front of a paper lunch bag. They then illustrate and cut out drawings that represent characters and elements of the setting that the readers believe will make the story more interesting to a listener.

When the visuals are completed, the storyteller stands behind the Paper Bag Theatre and begins telling the story while pulling out the appropriate visuals to support the story line.

Story Bag

Students collect realia representing key points in the story and place them in a bag. They then use these real items as storytelling props. For example, a Story Bag for Cinderella might have a cleaning rag, a high-heeled shoe, a pumpkin, and a clock.

Students create illustrations and gather artifacts that will assist them in retelling a story or content from a unit of study.

Sharing Paper Bag retells with an audience provide authentic purpose.

Storytelling at the Overhead

Students use overhead transparencies to draw the characters and setting elements from a favorite story. They then stand at the overhead to do their retelling, using the visuals they have created.

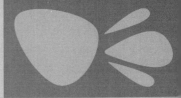

Storytelling Apron and Storytelling Vest

Younger students really enjoy wearing storytelling aprons, storytelling vests, and storytelling hats. The apron and vest can be made from felt with minimal amounts of sewing. The storytelling hat can be made by taking any suitable hat and covering the dome with sticky-back Velcro™ strips.

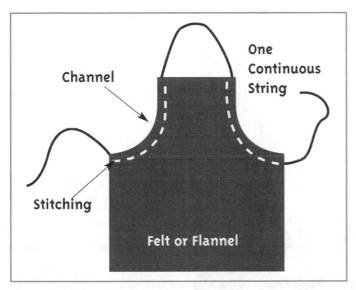

FIGURE 3–2 *Apron Pattern*

Students enjoy working in teams to create visuals for the storytelling apron.

The Process

Students draw the characters and props that they want to use in retelling a story on heavyweight tag paper. Then, they apply sticky-backed Velcro™ to the back of their illustrations. The illustrations should be large enough to be seen from several feet away. When they go to perform their retell, the students can wear their felt vest, apron, or hat and adhere their Velcro-backed art to the garment as they tell the story.

Storytelling vests are a great alternative to storytelling aprons.

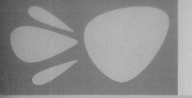

A Trick of the Hand

Hand Print Retells

Have students trace around their hands, making sure to go between each finger. Then on each finger of the tracing, students can write an element of story structure they want to remember in their retelling (e.g., the main idea).

A Trick of the Hand

Comprehension Strands	Level of Thinking	Action Vocabulary
Summarize	Organizing	Sequence, group
	Generating	Explain, elaborate

Storytelling Glove

Using newly purchased white garden gloves, write storytelling elements on each finger of the glove and place a heart in the center for the author's message. Students can then wear the glove while rehearsing for retelling.

Food handler's gloves can also be used for this purpose and are a very inexpensive way to provide parents with take-home versions of the Storytelling Glove.

Storytelling Gloves scaffold and support young learners by reminding them of key story elements.

Plain white gardening gloves are perfect for making Storytelling Gloves.

Compare and Contrast

Name of reader(s) _____ Date _____

Authors have different ways of utilizing story structure. Compare two books and consider the similarities and differences in the following areas.

	Book 1	**Book 2**
Title	_____	_____
	_____	_____
	_____	_____
The setting	_____	_____
	_____	_____
	_____	_____
The problem	_____	_____
	_____	_____
	_____	_____
The climax	_____	_____
	_____	_____
	_____	_____
The ending	_____	_____
	_____	_____
	_____	_____

Explain which book was your favorite and tell why.

_____

_____

_____

Varying Retells

Retells on Tape

Book reviews and retells can take many forms. One of my favorites is to invite students to make an audiotape of a retell for a favorite book and place it in a resealable bag that attaches to the inside cover of the book. Students who are book browsing and making selections of books to read can elect to listen to the retell as part of their process of deciding whether to read this book. Your students can turn this into a book review by including their opinions.

Varying Retells

Comprehension Strands	Level of Thinking	Action Vocabulary
Summarize	Integrating	Summarize information into cohesive statements
	Organizing	Sequence
Synthesize	Evaluating	Judge, assess
Use sensory imaging	Organizing	Represent, determine main ideas

Support Retell and Summary with Dramatic Interpretation

Dramatic interpretation engages students in total physical response as they use their bodies to portray the pathway of magma as it surges from deep in the earth to surface in an eruption, a bold journalist, or an emerging writer bristling with attitude. The use of physical motion to portray understanding activates many systems of understanding and supports long-term memory (Jensen 2008, Hoyt 1994).

Dramatic interactions support inference, interpretation, and critical thinking.

Eric Jensen's brain research reminds us that "motion equals memory" and has a significant impact on content retention.

Puppets can also support dramatic interpretation and increase reader engagement. I like to offer students a variety of puppet experiences, especially for students who are uncomfortable speaking in front of others.

Puppets scaffold engagement and motivation.

Spicing It Up with Line Drawings

Students who enjoy drawing often enjoy illustrating *while* they tell a story. They can stand in front of an easel with a felt pen and create line drawings as they talk about story elements. It also works well to have students stand at the chalkboard or at the overhead to draw as they retell.

Line drawings add visual support to concept attainment.

Props such as puppets and masks engage learners in shifting point of view and taking on the role of a character.

Cumulative Retells

This activity involves physical movement and lots of repetition. Like cumulative story structure, it is an add-on format in which everything that is already known is repeated each time a new element of the retell is added.

After reading a story, I ask a volunteer to come to the front of the room and "tell" the first event from the story. A second volunteer comes forward to tell the second event but before that person tells it, the first student repeats event #1. A cumulative retell for Cinderella might sound something like:

Step 1. Teller #1: Once upon a time there was a girl named Cinderella who lived with her stepmother and stepsisters.

Step 2. Teller #1: Once upon a time there was a girl named Cinderella who lived with her stepmother and stepsisters.

Teller #2: She had to clean and work and was called Cinderella because she had to clean the ashes out of the fireplace.

Step 3. Teller #1: Once upon a time there was a girl named Cinderella who lived with her stepmother and stepsisters.

Teller #2: She had to clean and work and was called Cinderella because she had to clean the ashes out of the fireplace.

Teller #3: The stepsisters were very excited because they were buying beautiful dresses to wear to a ball at the palace.

and so on.

The students love the repetition and the rhythm that develops as this process unfolds, and I find that challenged learners are especially supported by the fun-filled repetition of story elements. A variation to this would be to have audience members make up a physical action for each teller's event so they are physically involved even as listeners.

Vocabulary and content are well supported with cumulative retells.

Cumulative retells solidify understanding as retells "begin from the beginning" as new information is added.

Personal Reflection: Retelling Checklist

Name _____ Date _____

Story _____

Opening

☐ I began my retelling with an introduction.

Setting

☐ I included when and where the story happened.

Characters

☐ I told about the main character.

☐ I told about other characters.

Problem

☐ I told about the problem of the story.

Solution

☐ I told how the problem was solved.

☐ I told how the story ended.

Author's Message

☐ I shared my ideas about the author's message.

The best part of my retelling was _____

_____

The next time I retell, I need to remember _____

_____

My audience was _____

_____

Retelling: Self-Evaluation

Name _____

When I think about my retells, I know I am good at: _____

_____

_____

_____

_____

I am working on: _____

_____

_____

_____

_____

My goal as a storyteller is: _____

_____

_____

_____

_____

Retell Reflections: Self-Reflection

Reader _____ Story _____ Date _____

When I do a retell, I remember to:

	Yes	**I will try to remember next time**
Look at my audience.	☐	☐
Think about the story.	☐	☐
Speak clearly.		
Tell my favorite part and why I like it.	☐	☐
Include:		
The beginning of the story	☐	☐
The middle of the story	☐	☐
The ending	☐	☐
Characters	☐	☐
Setting	☐	☐
The problem	☐	☐

My rating of this story: It deserves _____ stars because _____

_____

_____

I am getting better at _____

I am going to work a little harder on _____

_____

_____

Scoring Guide: Reading Retell

6 **Characters**
Describes all main and secondary characters
Describes traits of main characters

Plot
Provides analysis, including inferences
Makes personal connections to the story
Retells main and secondary events in order with detail

Theme
Relates a message that demonstrates understanding of world issues

Setting
Includes specific details about place or time

Problem/Solution
Describes problem and resolution
Designates climax
May evaluate tension level

---

4 **Characters**
Identifies all main characters
Describes some character traits

Plot
Includes a description of key events in order
Includes main idea, beginning, middle, and end of story

Setting
Accurate information about time and place

Problem/Solution
Can identify problem and resolution

---

2 **Characters**
Names some characters

Plot
Limited summary
Limited understanding of author's message

Problem/Solution
Limited or missing

Teacher Checklist: Story Retelling

Student's Name _____ Date _____ Age/Grade _____

Title and Author of Book _____

	Minimum	Moderate	Excellent
1. Accurately retells literal information	☐	☐	☐
2. Includes inferred information	☐	☐	☐
3. Provides information about characters	☐	☐	☐
4. Describes the setting	☐	☐	☐
5. Includes a summary or a generalization	☐	☐	☐
6. Restates the problem and solution	☐	☐	☐
7. Makes evaluative statements or generates a question about the text	☐	☐	☐
8. Relates personal knowledge or or experience to the text	☐	☐	☐

Retelling Profile: Plot Structure

Teller _____ Date _____

Text _____ Listener _____

	Minimal Information			Very Complete	
Characters	1	2	3	4	5
Setting	1	2	3	4	5
Plot	1	2	3	4	5
Problem	1	2	3	4	5
Solution	1	2	3	4	5
Personal Inferences	1	2	3	4	5

Retelling Profile: Literary Elements

Teller _____ Date _____

Text _____ Listener _____

	Minimal Information			Very Complete	
Theme	1	2	3	4	5
Plot	1	2	3	4	5
Mood	1	2	3	4	5
Tension	1	2	3	4	5
Structure	1	2	3	4	5

Student Retell Record

Student: _____

Year: _____

+	Tells independently
P	Tells with prompting
P–	Prompted but still can't retell

Date	Story or Retell Activity	Uses Props	Characters	Identifies Main Character	Setting	Summarizes Plot	Describes Events — Beginning	Describes Events — Middle	Describes Events — End	Offers an Opinion/Evaluative Statement

Story Retell Directions: Tell about this book; pretend you are telling a friend about it who has never seen or heard it before. Did the story remind you of anything?

Classroom Retelling Profile

Key:

+ Information given without prompts
✓ Information given with prompts
0 Information not given

Student name	Book	Characters	Plot: Events	Theme	Setting	Problem/Solution

Data can be collected over multiple retellings. Patterns of performance can be easily detected in a particular dimension of the retell, such as character, plot, and so on.

Observation Guide

Name of child _____

This reflection completed by _____ Date _____

When listening to a story, my child:

	Usually	Sometimes	Rarely
Looks closely at the pictures	☐	☐	☐
Looks at or points to words	☐	☐	☐
Responds to the meaning by making comments, laughing, etc.	☐	☐	☐
Gives an opinion about the story	☐	☐	☐

When retelling a story, my child:

	Usually	Sometimes	Rarely
Speaks clearly and can be understood	☐	☐	☐
Uses eye contact with listeners	☐	☐	☐
Includes main events from the story	☐	☐	☐
Includes key characters	☐	☐	☐
Mentions the setting for the story	☐	☐	☐
Can tell about the problem in the story and how it was solved	☐	☐	☐

Parent Page: The Story Star

Retelling stories helps children understand books better. Please take a few minutes to invite your child to retell a story that you have shared together. As your child talks, you might want to be looking at the Story Star on page 109 to give your child clues about story components that may have been omitted. As your child gains confidence, you might ask your child to use the Story Star to plan a retell for you and/or the family, then "perform" when he or she is ready.

The Story Star

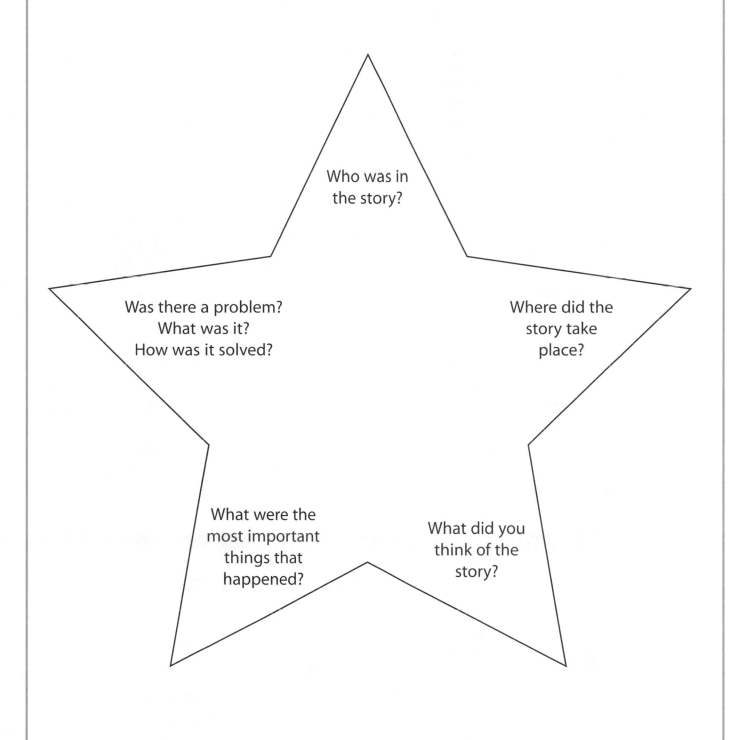

Who was in
the story?

Was there a problem?
What was it?
How was it solved?

Where did the
story take
place?

What were the
most important
things that
happened?

What did you
think of the
story?

CHAPTER 4 AT-A-GLANCE

Retelling Strategy	Comprehension Strands	Classification of Thinking	Page
If I Were the Author	Question	Analyzing	116
	Synthesize	Evaluating	
Book Rating and Book Review	Synthesize	Evaluating	118
	Summarize	Integrating	
Image Search: The Art of Good Writing	Use sensory imaging	Organizing	122
	Synthesize	Evaluating	
Interactive Journals	Determine importance	Knowing	126
	Connect	Generating	
		Integrating	
Writing Letters	Summarize	Organizing	129
Key Word Strategy	Summarize	Knowing	130
	Determine importance	Integrating	
	Infer	Analyzing	
Organizing a Summary	Summarize	Organizing	135
My Character Says	Synthesize	Generating	138
Story Reflections	Infer	Generating	139
	Use sensory imaging	Integrating	
Pass Around Retells	Summarize	Organizing	141
	Determine importance	Generating	
The Important Thing About…	Determine importance	Integrating	142
Creating a Readers Theatre Script	Determine importance	Applying	144
Attribute Graph	Synthesize	Evaluating	146
Sketch to Stretch	Use sensory imaging	Analyzing	148
	Summarize	Integrating	
Word Theatre	Use sensory imaging	Generating	150
	Infer	Analyzing	
Communicating Through Art	Summarize	Organizing	152
Character Analysis	Infer	Evaluating	153
Riddling Along	Question	Applying	154
	Connect	Knowing	
Dual Bio Poems	Connect	Organizing	156
Personal Narrative: Written Reflections	Summarize	Integrating	157

Written Reflections

When children write, they read. When children write, they think and reflect. When children write, they utilize all they know about sounds, symbols, the structures of language, and the construction of meaning (Calkins 2005). In an ideal language-learning classroom, children should be writing all day long. They should write to fulfill a basic human need for expression. They should write for the joy of it. They should write to remember. They should write in authentic, meaningful ways and then write some more.

Writing has been long understood as a tool for development of long-term memory and for deepening understanding. When the power of writing is combined with the power of analysis and reflection, students are immersed in a language-learning atmosphere that is charged with possibility. Writing develops both thinking and learning by creating a means for learners to modify and extend their understanding.

The structures that follow are designed to be *one small part* of a broad and richly developed classroom writing program.

Written Retells

Written retells are easy to prepare and naturally accommodate all developmental levels; they are perfect vehicles for increasing learner responsibility while deepening understanding of published and student-authored texts (Hoyt 1999). They assist learners in fine-tuning their understanding of text structure, while enhancing their achievements as readers and writers. In their dual role as instructional and assessment tools, written retells and summaries can be analyzed for a wide range of understandings about the text and the writer's understanding of written language.

A kindergartner's advice on writing well:
1. *Use your words.*
2. *Take a deep breath.*
3. *Whack away.*

Written retells support content retention and acquisition of academic vocabulary.

Some other sample written retells:

The moon shines on the Earth.

Making a Peanut Butter and Jelly Sandwich

You need to get the peanut butter, jelly, two pieces of bread, and knife out. Spread the peanut butter on one piece of bread. Spread the jelly on top of the peanut butter. Put the other piece of bread on top of all of that. Cut the sandwich into pieces. Eat!

Making a Sandwich

A True American Hero
The Story of Rosa Parks

A Tired Woman Trying to Get Home
She wasn't a tall woman or a loud woman. She wasn't a woman who made a scene. She was a tired woman, riding a bus, heading home after a long days work. As the bus filled up, Rosa Parks sat quietly, resting her tired feet and anticipating the relief of relaxing at home.

An Unreasonable Demand
As was common in those days, the bus driver told her that she needed to give up her seat to a white man. He expected this quiet black woman to follow his order, figuring that no black person would face a jail sentence over a bus seat. He was wrong.

Taking a Stand
Mrs. Parks decided to stand up for her rights by remaining seated. She was arrested and sent to jail for simply sitting in her seat.

Changing the Future
While Rosa Parks did have to stand trial, her courage sparked others, such as Martin Luther King, Jr., to cry out against such unfair treatment. The result was that laws were changed and everyone had a chance to be truly equal. Rosa Parks, a true American hero.

A True American Hero

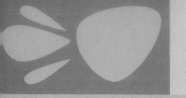

If I Were the Author

If I Were the Author engages students in critical/analytical reflections as they consider attributes of a selection that they would affirm and celebrate, then consider ways in which the selection could have been improved.

If I Were the Author

Comprehension Strands	Level of Thinking	Action Vocabulary
Question	Analyzing	Analyze, identify characteristics
Synthesize	Evaluating	Judge, evaluate, assess

In reflecting on *fiction*, readers might consider the way the selection:

✱ develops rich and strong characters

✱ integrates sensory imaging

✱ draws the reader into the action and the setting

✱ develops mood and tension

✱ brings out the voice of the author

✱ utilizes action verbs

✱ captures the reader's attention with the lead

✱ creates a satisfying conclusion

✱ sets up the problem and resolution

✱ utilizes rich vocabulary

✱ varies sentence structures to create sentence fluency and a pleasing cadence

✱ is narrated (consider point of view)

✱ communicates the author's purpose

In reflecting on *nonfiction*, readers might consider:

✱ strategies the author uses to draw the reader into the selection

✱ WOW power of visuals and language

✱ the way visuals and text work together to create a strong message

✱ the accuracy of information

✱ concept development (Are ideas fully explained?)

✱ the author's point of view

✱ word choice

✱ use of strong verbs and sensory imaging

✱ organization

✱ use of text features such as headings, captions, labels, and bold text

✱ the author's purpose

✱ how well the lead engages the reader

✱ the quality of the closing (Did it provide a summary, an invitation to learn more, or leave the reader feeling dissatisfied?)

✱ descriptions

✱ whether the piece is factual or persuasive

Critical analysis begins with taking a step back from the print and considering ways in which it could be improved.

Students gather sentences to serve as exemplars for their own writing and to use in If I Were the Author conversations.

Critical/analytical reflections must be built upon a base of extensive reading in a wide variety of text types.

Submitting the work of well-respected authors to critical analysis heightens understanding of craft and deepens comprehension.

If I Were Author

Name _____ Date _____

Book Title _____ Author _____

Things about this book/story that I would be proud of

_____

_____

_____

_____

_____

_____

_____

Things about this book/story that I would change

_____

_____

_____

_____

_____

_____

_____

Things I learned about the author's style of writing that I could use in my own writing

_____

_____

_____

_____

_____

_____

_____

If I were to talk about this book with a friend, I would be sure to point out

_____

_____

_____

_____

_____

_____

_____

These are alternative forms to consider as you engage students in critical analysis of reading selections. They both engage readers in offering opinions about their reading. What is important is that learners offer options that they can justify with specific examples. Additional ideas for book reviews are located in Chapter 2, page 28–29.

Book Rating and Book Review

Comprehension Strands	Level of Thinking	Action Vocabulary
Synthesize	Evaluating	Judge, evaluate, assess
Summarize	Integrating	Connect and combine, cohesive statements

Borders Book Reviews

Borders Books, like many other bookstores, produces a newsletter profiling activities and new books on the market. In Beaverton, Oregon, Borders invites students from local schools to write reviews and then the student-authored reviews are published in the newsletter!

Are you curious?

The Best Book Grant's Read Recently

Winner of the 1997 Oregon Book Award for Fiction and soon to be a motion picture, **Fight Club** is not a new book, but it is one of the best books I've read recently.

The narrator of **Fight Club** is an investigator for an automobile insurance company. His job is to decide whether it is financially better for his company to issue recalls or to ignore a car's defects and pay the inevitable injury & death lawsuits. To give himself a perspective on life & death, he regularly attends group meetings for the terminally ill (although he has no illness). This suits him until he meets Tyler Durden - a man with a very different philosophy of life. Tyler changes our narrators life completely - beginning a downward spiral that leads to an unpredictable ending.

With **Fight Club**, we are introduced to the unique style of Portland author **Chuck Palahniuk**. The story constantly surprises, and the writing pulls you on until the remarkable ending. Palahniuk is somehow able to create a rhythm with his writing but doesn't allow it to become predictably patterned. I never read anything quite like **Fight Club**!

Note: **Fight Club** will be discussed at our March Original Book Discussion Group.

Kids' Stuff

Book Reviews by Students From William Walker Elementary

I loved **So Far From Home** by **Barry Kenenberg**. It is my favorite book because I couldn't put it down. I read it to my sister every night before I went to bed. I even read it at the dentist's office before I went in for my checkup.

This book is different because it is in diary form. The diary is written by Mary Driscoll, a young Irish girl. She wrote in this journal almost every day unless she was sick. The story started out in Skibbereen County cork, Ireland in 1847. Mary's family is about to loose their home because they don't have any money for food. So, her Aunt Nora sends her a ticket to Lowell, Massachusetts. In order to get to America she has to sail on a ship across the Atlantic Ocean. She is on the ship for twenty-eight days and many interesting things happen to her.

To find out what happens to Mary and who she meets in America, you'll have to read **So Far From Home**, one of the books from the *Dear America Series*. It was terrific! You won't regret it!
- by Natasha Myrdahl

Sweet Valley High: Jessica's First Kiss by **Francine Pascal** was a great book! I read it every night. In fact, sometimes I read for hours because I wanted to know what was going to happen next.

The story took place at a campsite in the woods in the Nineties. The main characters, Jessica and Elizabeth, are identical twin sisters and they don't like each other very much. The girls decide to go on a camping trip with their eight grade class. Everybody has to have a partner and the girls get stuck with each other. This is where it starts getting interesting. As the girls are roasting marshmallows, Their boyfriends show up. Jessica likes Elizabeth's boyfriend Dennis, so she starts confusing the boys. Todd ends up thinking that Elizabeth is his girlfriend and Dennis is Jessica's boyfriend. Elizabeth fights back but to find out how, you'll have to read this book!

Gifts For Your Valentine

The 50 Most Romantic Things Ever Done
by Dini Von Mueffling

A Reasonable Affliction: 1001 Love Poems to Read to Each Other
edited by Sally Ann Berk & James Gordon Wakeman

Inter Courses: An Aphrodisiac Cookbook
by Martha Hopkins & Randall Lockridge

101 Nights of Grrreat Romance
by Laura Corn

The Art of Kissing
by William Cane

Weekends For Two In the Pacific Northwest: 50 Romantic Getaways
by Bill Gleeson

Staff Selections

New books that our employees believe deserve extra attention; they will be discounted 30% for the month.

Clone: the Road to Dolly
by Gina Kolata

Repent Harlequin! Said Ticktockman
by Harlan Ellison

Barney's Version
by Mordecai Richler

The Climb: Tragic Ambition on Mt. Everest
by Anatoli Boukreev

Conquest of Cool
by Thomas Frank

I usually watch the *Sweet Valley High* television show but I liked this book so much, I am going to read more of the books in the *Sweet Valley Twins* series instead.
- by Ashley Davis

Borders Book, Music, & Cafe, 2605 SW Cedar Hills Blvd., Beaverton, OR 97005 • (503) 644-6164

FIGURE 4–1 *Borders Book Review*

Book Rating

Student _____ Date _____

The Book _____ Author _____

This book was:

☐ So good I couldn't put it down

☐ Pretty interesting

☐ OK

☐ Not great

I rated the book this way because:

If I were to pass this book along to a friend, I would say:

Book Review: Narrative

Name_____ Date _____

Title of book _____ Author _____

Illustrator_____

My opinion of the story:

My opinion of the illustrations:

My recommendations to others about this book:

My Favorites

Name _____ Date _____

Of all the books I have read, _____ has the best beginning.

The author is _____

I liked the beginning because _____

_____

_____

Of all the books I have read, _____ has the best middle.

The author is _____

I liked the middle because _____

_____

_____

Of all the books I have read, _____ has the best ending.

The author is _____

I liked the ending because _____

_____

_____

Image Search: The Art of Good Writing

When learners compare and contrast passages, they are challenged to look for similarities and differences. They push themselves to search for excellence in exemplars that match up to the attributes they most value in writing. This effort to determine importance in exemplars deepens comprehension and clarifies the attributes we most value in written text.

When students first attempt an Image Search, I narrow the focus by asking them to find mentor books that have the most interesting characters. We search for books with richly developed characters then engage in conversations about what makes a character interesting. What does the author do to develop a character so fully that we understand what they are like and can visualize them as a person? This leads to rich conversations about why these particular books were found to be the *best* in character development. As the conversation and examples are shared, create a class list of attributes of strong character development.

Once students learn the process, you can have them search for books in which sensory imaging brings the setting to life—books with fantastic photographs that bring you into the scene or situation, books with rich vocabulary that supports visualization, and so on. In each search, students discuss, share their exemplars, and create a list of attributes that will support further searches and empower their writing.

Image Search The Art of Good Writing

Comprehension Strands	Level of Thinking	Action Vocabulary
Use sensory imaging	Organizing	Classify, compare
Synthesize	Evaluating	Rate judge

As with all other strategies, independence is scaffolded with a series of careful think-alouds in which I model the process. Steps may include the following:

✷ Collaborate with students to create a list of what to look for when identifying outstanding sensory images in a mentor text. What are the attributes that help us to visualize?

✷ Model how to review familiar books, skimming and scanning for evidence of an attribute. Show students how to record sensory sentences on sentence strips.

✷ Think aloud after reading a short passage, opening a pathway to your thinking about a selection and the sensory images you are able to develop.

In an Image Search, readers learn to select specific examples of excellence, comparing and contrasting their examples with those of their conversation partners.

Image Search conversations are a rich mix of reading exemplar passages aloud and discussion.

Students share their selections from an Image Search.

Image Search: The Art of Good Writing

Name _____ Date _____

Please select three books that you are familiar with and either reread them or skim through them, searching for points where the author has used descriptive language to build strong visual images. Please use sticky notes to mark your favorite points in each book, then choose the *very best* example from each book. After you make your selections, think about how you will share them with others. You may want to practice reading them aloud with expression or think of how you can help others develop an appreciation for the rich language in your samples.

Example #1: From (book) _____ by _____

This excerpt came from page: _____

I selected this because _____

Example #2: From (book) _____ by _____

This excerpt came from page: _____

I selected this because _____

Example #3: From (book) _____ by _____

This excerpt came from page: _____

I selected this because _____

What did you learn about descriptive writing?

How will you change your own writing as a result of what you learned?

Focus on Emotions

The Reader/Writer _____

The Book _____

Significant Emotions in This Book

My Reflections/Observations
How were these emotions made clear? What did the author do to develop the reader's understanding? Show examples of the author's craft.

1. _____   _____

_____

_____

2. _____   _____

_____

_____

3. _____   _____

_____

_____

Response Points

✳ What did I learn about the craft of writing?

✳ How can I use this in my writing today and in the future?

Quotables

Name_____ Date _____

Book Title _____ Author _____

Skim through your book and search for three quotes that are especially significant. These quotes might be selected because they offer outstanding descriptions, give deeper insight into a character, foreshadow an upcoming problem, represent an important moment in the story, or represent a moment when you personally felt connected to the story or to a character. As you select your quotes, think about how you could explain their importance to someone else.

Quote #1	Why I chose it
_____	_____
_____	_____
_____	_____

Quote #2	Why I chose it
_____	_____
_____	_____
_____	_____

Quote #3	Why I chose it
_____	_____
_____	_____
_____	_____

Interactive Journals

Interactive Journals engage students in written conversations that facilitate critical/analytical thinking while casting students as active respondents to writing partners. Like a literature circle in which the participants write, rather than talk, Interactive Journals challenge students to reach deep within themselves as they summarize, offer opinions, support their thinking, and learn to respond to others' thoughts.

Interactive Journals

Comprehension Strands	Level of Thinking	Action Vocabulary
Determine importance	Knowing	Identify, clarify
Connect	Generating	Conclude, explain, elaborate
	Integrating	Connect and combine, summarize, generalize

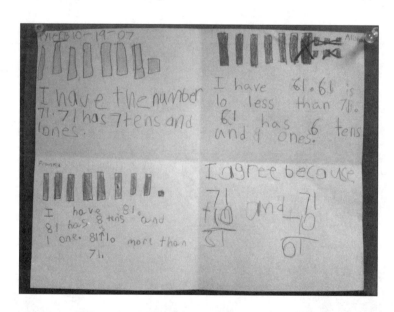

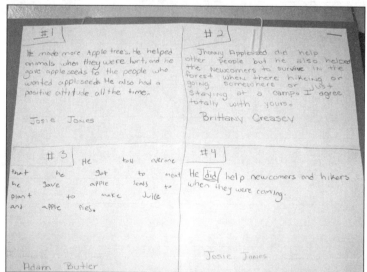

Interactive journals encourage full participation. All students write in quadrant #1. Then, papers are passed. Team members read #1 and write in quadrant #2.

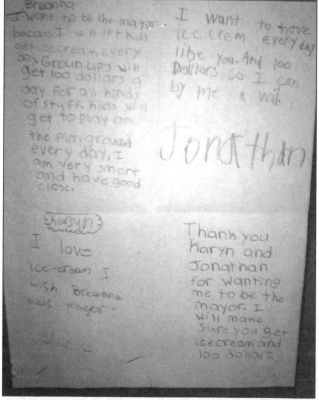

At a signal from the teacher or a discussion leader, papers are again passed. Team members read #1 and #2 and write in #3.

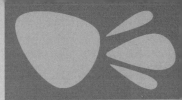

For Emergent Writers

Materials a large sheet of paper folded in half for every student

Step #1. Each student draws and writes about a story or learning experience using one half of the paper.

Step #2. Partners talk about their drawing, their writing, and their reflections.

Step #3. The partners trade papers.

Step #4. Using the second section on their partner's paper, each student draws and writes a response to their partner's work. This might take the form of adding information, voicing a shared thought about the story, or something else.

Step #5. Sharing. Partners meet in larger groups to talk about their shared drawing and writing.

Emergent writers can utilize interactive journals when they combine drawing and writing to express their thinking.

Responses to The Very Hungry Caterpillar

For More Fluent Writers

Materials 8.5-×-11-inch paper, folded into fourths, then opened flat. Number the quadrants 1 through 4. This works best immediately following a learning opportunity such as reading, discussing, or problem solving.

Step #1. Students gather in teams of three. Each team member has his or her own paper and pencil or pen. They need to know that there will be an audience for their writing as other members of their group will read and respond to what they write.

Step #2. All students begin writing and reflecting in quadrant #1. Their writing might be stimulated with questions such as, "What did you think about the story?" "What personal connections were there for you?" "What is the most important thought to remember about the Civil War?" and so on.

Step #3. At a predetermined signal, have the students pass their papers within their group. (I usually have everyone pass to the right to avoid confusion.) They now are holding someone else's paper. The task is to read what is written in quadrant #1 and then respond in quadrant #2 with additional thoughts, reactions, or shared feelings.

Step #4. The students pass their papers one more time. This time they read quadrant #1 and quadrant #2, then respond in #3.

Step #5. All papers return to their original owners. The owner of the paper reads all responses and then reflects in quadrant #4. This self-reflection might include thoughts such as "Do I still feel the same as I did in quadrant #1?" "Did I learn anything new?" "What lingering questions do I have?"

An Interactive Journal scaffolds deep thinking about civil rights and racism.

Example

#1 Evan

I don't think the drinking age should be lowered to 18. The papers are full of stories about teenagers in car accidents because they have been drinking. It doesn't make sense to make the problem worse.

#2 Marcus

I see your point about driving but it also doesn't make sense to me that an 18-year-old can go in the army and be old enough to vote but can't drink legally.

#3 Juan

I think that the driving age should be changed too. Maybe there are so many teenage accidents because teenagers just aren't ready to drive. My brother drives but he isn't responsible enough to do his homework.

#4 Evan

I wonder if there should be one age for everything. Voting, driving, and legal drinking should happen when you can act and think like an adult. I wonder what age would be best.

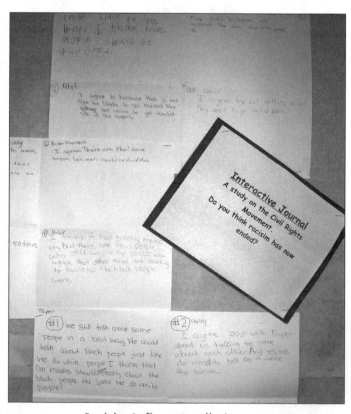

Writing Letters

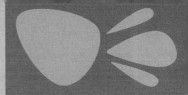

Students who write letters to show what they know have an opportunity to explore their own meanings, express themselves through written language, and engage in social dialogue, all while practicing a genre that is useful throughout life.

Here are examples from a health class:

Example

Dear Jenny,

Did you know that babies have 300 bones in their bodies? I have been reading about the human body, and I learned that bones grow together so that when you are older you only have 206 bones.

I also learned that the center of our bones makes our red blood cells. Red blood cells carry oxygen and give us energy.

Megan

Example

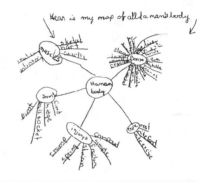

Here is an example from a math class:

Example

Dear Mom,

We are learning about fractions. At first I thought they were hard but then the teacher brought in apples and candy bars. We cut them into parts and had to tell how much we were eating. I got to eat 1/6 of an apple and 1/4 of a candy bar. I guess fractions aren't so hard.

Love,
Kyle

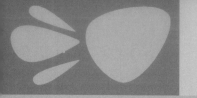

Key Word Strategy

The Key Word Strategy is one that should reside in a prominent place on the tool-belt of every reader. Key words can be drawn from fiction or nonfiction, relate to characters, setting, or any number of under-standings that are central to comprehension. The significance of this strategy lies in the ability of a reader to extract key words, then set the text aside and use the key words to create an oral or written summary.

Students begin by selecting words that are present in the reading, gathering the words that they believe are key to understanding the passage. Ideally, the key words appear as bold-faced text in the writing; students can then easily create their list of key words based on those highlighted words. When words are emphasized in the text this way, it gives a strong message to the reader that these key words are important and are worthy of special attention.

Selected words are written on sticky notes and placed on the page or aligned beside the book. After reading, the student closes his or her book, arranges the key words in an order that supports a cohesive summary, and then retells or writes to summarize.

Key Word Strategy

Comprehension Strands	Level of Thinking	Action Vocabulary
Summarize	Knowing	Choose, store for recall
Determine importance	Integrating	Connect and combine, summarize into cohesive statements
Infer	Analyzing	Determine importance, infer

Key words appear in bold in this second grade writing sample.

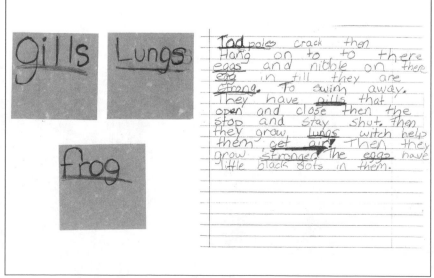

The key word, protect, appears in the heading and as boldface text in Madison's summary.

Students write key words on sticky notes, then use the key words to write summaries.

Revisit, Reflect, Retell ✳ UPDATED EDITION

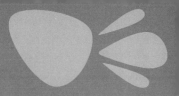

Inferring with Key Words

Once students catch on to extracting literal-level key words from the selection, they can then shift to selecting key words that are inferences about a text.

Example #1

After reading *Mrs. Wishy Washy*, a student might select a key word such as *determined*. *Determined* does not appear in the text, but a strong argument could be made that Mrs. Wishy-Washy is determined to get those animals clean.

Example #2

After reading the scene in *Hatchet* where Brian attempts to land the airplane, students might select inferential key words such as *courage*, *terrified*, or *focused*. These words do not appear in the chapter, but they would be excellent inferences about Brian's situation.

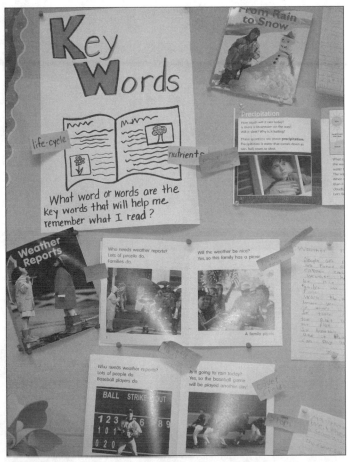

Students write key words on sticky notes.

Students display the key words they have selected from their reading.

A student from Howard County, Maryland uses the Key Word Strategy to support content retention.

Kindergarten students use key words and art to support writing.

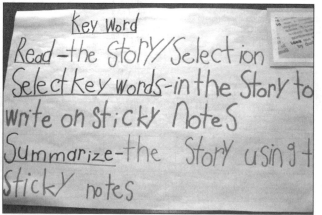

Middle School students may elect to use a two-column format with key words on the left and summaries on the right.

Students at Reeds Elementary in North Carolina create charts outlining the steps of the Key Word Strategy.

Key Word Strategy

1. Read a selection.

2. Reread it with the goal of trying to select a few key words that seem especially important. Write these words on sticky notes. Be selective. You want **most important** words.

3. Arrange the words in a way that supports you as you retell the story in your head. (For example, in Cinderella *fireplace* and *cinders* would probably come before *pumpkin*.)

4. Use your words to get you started writing a summary of the story. Be sure to underline or bold your key words.

The Reader _____ Date _____

The Book _____

Key Word List

My summary:

How many of your key words appeared in your summary?

Point It Out!

The Reader/Writer _____

The Book _____

Identify key words and phrases that, in very few words, bring about strong visual images.

Key Words and Phrases   **Produces strong images about:**

1. _____   _____

2. _____   _____

3. _____   _____

4. _____   _____

5. _____   _____

6. _____   _____

7. _____   _____

8. _____   _____

Share your choices and tell *why* you selected them.

Response Points

✳ What did I learn about the craft of writing?

✳ How can I use this in my writing today and in the future?

Organizing a Summary

This is about: ☐ a book ☐ a real event

Writer _____ Date _____

1. Draw a picture of one main idea in each of the boxes below.
2. Cut out the boxes and glue them on a large sheet of paper.
3. Draw arrows between the boxes to show the order.
4. Write about each picture.
5. Tell someone about your work. Be sure to tell why you chose the parts you selected.

Story Scaffold

Name of Student _____

Title of Story _____

The story begins when _____

_____

_____

The problem is _____

_____

_____

The next thing that happens is _____

_____

_____

Then _____

_____

_____

After that, _____

_____

_____

The problem is solved when _____

_____

_____

Preparing an Informational Summary

Reader _____ Title of book _____

Topic _____

* Create an illustration that shows what you learned in this book. Create labels to show the important parts. You may want to add a caption, too.

* Tell a partner about your illustration. Make sure your partner learns what you did.

My partner's name is _____

Key points to share:

-

-

-

-

* Write about your topic. Be sure to include the important ideas.

_____

_____

_____

_____

_____

My Character Says

Knowing that comprehension deepens significantly when a reader can experience understanding from multiple perspectives, My Character Says is designed as a strategy to help learners examine a character or historical figure in greater depth. Students work in teams of two, each choosing to become a different character from a story or historical event. They share one piece of paper.

One student opens by writing a question for the other to answer. There should be no talking!

Writers take on the role of a character from a book and engage in a written conversation.

Example #1 Responding to Little Red Riding Hood

Hi, Mr. Wolf. What are you doing?
I am going into the forest.
Oh, that's nice.
Where are you going?
To my Grandma's house.
OK Bye.
Goodbye!
Wait. What do you have in the basket?
Some treats for my Grandma.

Example #2 Responding to The Sign of the Beaver

Hey Matt. Why do you look at books and paper when you could be out hunting?
I like to read. I learn about places I have never visited and I learn how to do things.
Would you like me to teach you to read, Attean?
Yes. I would like to learn white man's book words.

My Character Says can engage writers in deep thinking about characters from history as well as from fiction.

Story Reflections

Draw a picture about the story.

_____
One word about the main character

_____ , _____
Two words describing the setting

_____ , _____ , _____
Three words telling the problem

_____ , _____ , _____ , _____
Four words about an event

_____ , _____ , _____ , _____ , _____
Five words about the solution

Terquain

Reader _____

Draw a picture about a book, a special character, or something you are learning about.

Follow the steps below to create a three-line poem.

_____

The Topic

_____ , _____ , _____
Two or Three Words About the Topic

_____
A Feeling or Synonym Related to the Topic

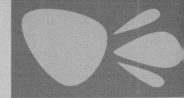

Pass Around Retells

Pass Around Retells

Students meet in teams of three or four. Each person has their own sheet of paper. At a signal, everyone begins writing a retell of the story on their own paper. When a timer rings, the papers are passed to the right. Each writer now has someone else's paper. The task is to read what has been written so far and continue the story from that point. When the timer rings again, the papers pass once more and the writing goes on. I find that students really appreciate the various points of view and do some in-depth thinking about which elements of a retell are really critical.

Pass Around Retells		
Comprehension Strands	**Level of Thinking**	**Action Vocabulary**
Summarize	Organizing	Sequence, explain
Determine importance	Generating	Elaborate

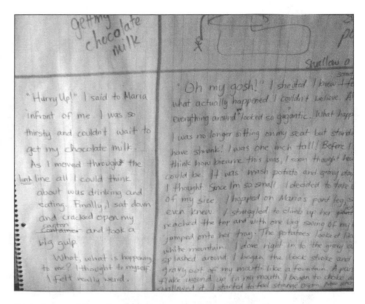

Pass Around Retells stimulate reflection on details, sequence, and main ideas.

In a Pass Around Retell, team members begin writing at a signal from the teacher or a leader. When the next signal is given, everyone passes their paper to the right, reads what the previous person wrote, and continues to write a retell of the story from wherever the last person stopped.

After the Pass Around Retell, team members talk about their retells, discussing strategies to write concise summaries, clarifying points of confusion, and asking questions of other writers.

The Important Thing About . . .

This structure helps students focus on main ideas and works equally well with a wide range of textual understandings. Students can use this to consider an entire story, a key character, a literary device used in the story, a person in their lives, or other themes.

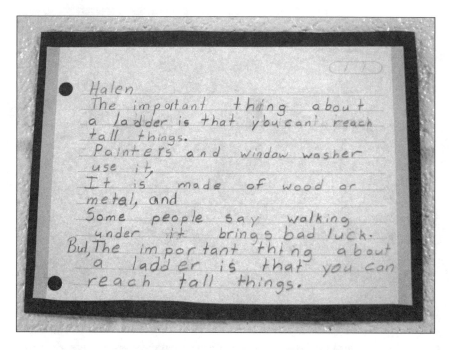

The Important Thing About . . . supports main idea and the development of a topic sentence and supporting details.

The Important Thing About . . .

Writer ____ Date ______________

Topic ____

The important thing about ____

is that ____

____

____

____

It is true that ____

____

____

____

But, the important thing about ____

is that ____

____

____

____

____

Adapted from *The Important Book* by Margaret Wise Brown.

Creating a Readers Theatre Script

Readers theatre scripts are powerful tools for helping students to read and write reflectively. To create a script, writers must read carefully, weighing critical points against those less worthy of attention. They then need to craft language that sounds fluent when read aloud. They also need to stretch into inferential reasoning to determine how voices should sound and how a narrator might assist the mood through carefully chosen comments.

Creating a Readers Theatre Script

Comprehension Strand	Level of Thinking	Action Vocabulary
Determine importance	Applying	Use information in a new context

Scripts for Expository Learning

The following example came from a fourth-grade student. He was asked to write a report about Abraham Lincoln, and he promptly began groaning and exhibiting every avoidance behavior he had in his bag of tricks. When the assignment was reconfigured to "Write a readers theatre script that you can perform with two friends," he was suddenly filled with enthusiasm and eagerly began researching and writing. What a change!

Performing readers theatre scripts in small teams engages all students in the action, maximizing time with text.

Example

Abraham Lincoln by Brenden

NARRATOR #1: In 1890 Abraham Lincoln was born in a log cabin in Kentucky. He moved a lot as a child.

NARRATOR #2: When he was nine, his mother, and her aunt, and her uncle died leaving his father to take care of Abe, his sister, and his second cousin.

NARRATOR #1: A year later, Abe's father left on a trip and the kids were left at home for many weeks.

EVERYONE: When his father returned, he had a new wife.

NARRATOR #2: Abraham worked hard to learn to read and write. He was also a hard laborer. He cut wood and even worked on the Mississippi River.

Readers theatre scripts created by students enhance content retention, expand writing proficiency, and improve reading fluency.

Engage students as writers and then as performers, sharing their readers theatre retellings of favorite stories and nonfiction explorations.

Scripts for Novels and Picture Books

To create readers theatre scripts with novels or picture books, students review the text to determine which events were most critical to the story line. They then review the narration and dialogue for each event and select the critical portions. It helps to work with photocopies of the text when they are at this stage so they can cross out and highlight as they discuss. Finally, they write their summaries of the dialogue and narration into a script.

Example

Cinderella by Megan

STEPMOTHER: Cinderella! Get in here right now. The prince is about to arrive with the glass slipper for your sisters to try on and this place is a mess!

CINDERELLA: Yes. Of course I will help you.

NARRATOR #1: She said in a sweet and patient voice.

NARRATOR #2: As Cinderella entered the room, her hand closed around the glass slipper that was tucked safely into her apron pocket.

STEPMOTHER: While you are cleaning, be sure to start a fire and then hurry quickly to start a pot of tea. It is very important that you get done and get back to the kitchen with the cook. We wouldn't want you in the way when the prince arrives.

NARRATOR #1: She said with a sneer.

Props such as hats, pin-on signs, and puppets enhance readers theatre experiences.

Attribute Graph

Attribute Graph

Comprehension Strand	Level of Thinking	Action Vocabulary
Synthesize	Evaluating	Judge, rate, assess

Work with the students to select a focus for this interaction. The focus might be attributes of a character, an author, a historical figure, the climax of a story, and so on.

Students discuss the attributes graph and list the attributes they agree to be most significant and/or well developed at the bottom of the graph. They then evaluate each attribute on a scale of 1 to 10.

Example

Attribute Graph for *Cinderella*

	Kind	Thoughtful	Creative	Generous	Wicked	Mean	Hardworking		
10	▓	▓					▓		
9	▓	▓					▓		
8	▓	▓					▓		
7	▓	▓					▓		
6	▓	▓					▓		
5	▓	▓		▓			▓		
4	▓	▓		▓			▓		
3	▓	▓		▓			▓		
2	▓	▓		▓			▓		
1	▓	▓		▓			▓		
Attributes	Kind	Thoughtful	Creative	Generous	Wicked	Mean	Hardworking		

Attribute Graph

Name_____

Attribute Analysis for _____

10								
9								
8								
7								
6								
5								
4								
3								
2								
1								
Attributes								

Sketch to Stretch

Sketch to Stretch is well worth bringing into our repertoire of comprehension-building strategies, as it can be so helpful to students who need support with visualization. I begin by modeling with an informational read-aloud, pausing often to create simple line drawings with labels to capture my learning up to that point. As I sketch, I think out loud about key ideas and how these drawings can help me to remember them.

The emphasis is on thinking, not art, so I am careful to use only one color if ink or pencil. As I draw, I express my delight in drawing arrows, squiggles, or rough representations of things. I repeatedly remind the students that this isn't supposed to be pretty. The idea is to use the sketches as tools for holding onto the content!

Sketch to Stretch		
Comprehension Strands	**Level of Thinking**	**Action Vocabulary**
Use sensory imaging	Analyzing	Diagram, examine
Summarize	Integrating	Imagine, connect and combine, cohesive statements

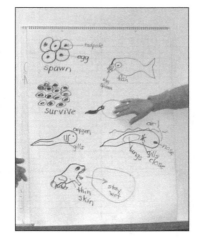

Sketches and labels assist with content retention.

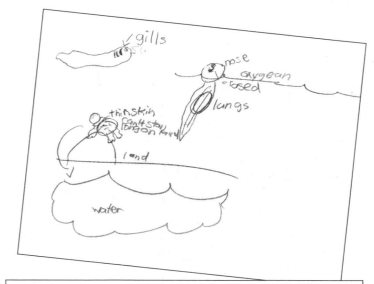

Two examples of student Sketch to Stretch and the writing that accompanied them.

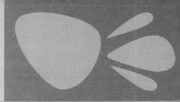

After sketching, students share and explain their drawings in small groups. Their sharing should focus on why they drew what they did and what they attempted to represent. The verbal explanation and the resulting conversations are more important to extending understanding than the sketch. The sketch is a vehicle for collecting thoughts and rehearsing for the conversation.

After guided practice and teacher modeling, students can transfer Sketch to Stretch into their independent reading as a scaffold to comprehension and writing.

Some students benefit from being asked an open-ended question such as: What did you learn? What did this mean to you? What did it make you think about? What key ideas stayed with you? or What did you think was the most significant part of the story?

Then, have students write. The academic language and concepts will flow easily on the foundation of sketching and talking.

This strategy is especially powerful for students who may be challenged with literacy learning as it provides much-needed quiet time. The drawing provides a quiet atmosphere during which all students can collect their thoughts about their reading and increases the likelihood that all can contribute to the discussion.

After sharing within groups, each group can select a sketch to share with the whole group or focus on a unifying theme that was present in all of their sketches.

A study of the human body is supported by Sketch to Stretch.

Students identify Sketch to Stretch as a strategy that helps them remember

The Role of the Teacher

✳ Demonstrate the process

✳ Be a partner. Model by creating a sketch and talking about it.

✳ Encourage students to talk about their reactions to their reading.

✳ Stimulate conversation about personal meanings the students have constructed related to the reading.

This strategy works well with all genres. In addition to high-quality literature, you may want to consider using current events in the newspaper; poetry; science experiments; concepts in social studies, health, math; or as a prewriting experience.

Students draw and write to capture important ideas.

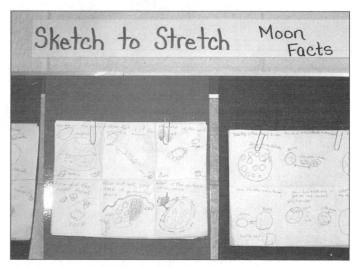

Sketch to Stretch is linked to key questions students will use to guide their research and writing.

Adapted from M. Seigel (1984).

Word Theatre

In Word Theatre, readers work in teams of two or three to reflect on a text they have just read. They select three or four words that they found to be particularly interesting or important in their reading and record them on the form.

It is important to note the page number from the text, so students can easily return to the context in which the word occurred.

After listing words and page numbers, the readers work in pairs or groups of three, and challenge themselves to dramatize each word in such a way that observers can guess the word. When the teams are ready, they direct their observers to turn to the page in the text where their word appears. The observers watch the dramatization of the word, then skim the page to try to locate what they believe to be the target word. When the observers think they have

found the word, they read the entire sentence in which the word appears, rather than simply shouting out the word. The dramatic team then confirms or clarifies the guess made by the observers.

After words have been dramatized, I challenge students to use their target words in their writing. This brings rich vocabulary onto the page and helps students to integrate the vocabulary and related concepts into long-term memory.

Word Theatre

Comprehension Strands	Level of Thinking	Action Vocabulary
Use sensory imaging	Generating	Produce new understanding
Infer	Analyzing	Infer, elaborate

Word theatre teaches students to reach deeply for the meaning behind a word, building context through dramatic interpretation.

Word Theatre

Actors _____

The book _____

1. Focus word: _____ **Selected from page** _____

Plan for dramatizing: _____

_____

The word means _____
_____

2. Focus word: _____ **Selected from page** _____

Plan for dramatizing: _____

_____

The word means _____
_____

3. Focus word: _____ **Selected from page** _____

Plan for dramatizing: _____

_____

The word means _____
_____

Communicating Through Art

Artist _____ Date _____

Book _____

Draw about the story and be ready to tell someone what you know. Later, you can cut these pictures apart, paste each one on a piece of paper, and then write about the pictures.

First
┌───┐
│   │
│   │
│   │
│   │
│   │
└───┘

Then
┌───┐
│   │
│   │
│   │
│   │
│   │
└───┘

Also
┌───┐
│   │
│   │
│   │
│   │
└───┘

Finally
┌───┐
│   │
│   │
│   │
│   │
└───┘

Character Analysis

Character Analysis for (name of character) _____

Name of Book _____ Reader/Writer _____

	Strength	**Weakness**	**Why**
Listening	☐	☐	_____
			_____
Facing challenges	☐	☐	_____
			_____
Solving problems	☐	☐	_____
			_____
Being creative	☐	☐	_____
			_____
Demonstrating patience	☐	☐	_____
			_____
Getting along with others	☐	☐	_____

This character's greatest strengths _____

_____

_____

_____

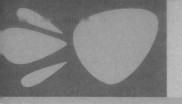

Riddling Along

Students love riddles and jokes and often enjoy creating riddles about characters, key events, or information gained from a unit of study.

Example

Focus on a character

She was pretty

She worked hard.

She had two stepsisters who were mean to her.

She had a fairy godmother.

She went to a ball and lost her glass slipper.

When it turned midnight, she ran home in rags.

Who is it?

Answer: _____

Focus on a unit of study

This animal has a large pouch under its beak.

It can scoop up a fish and carry it inside the pouch.

Answer: _____

Riddling Along

Topic for my riddle _____ _____

Name of author _____ Date _____

1. List facts you know on this topic:

2. Number your facts. Number 1 should be the fact least likely to give away the answer to your riddle. The highest number should go to the fact that would most likely give away the answer.

3. Rewrite the facts in the order you chose (Numbers 1 to ___) and think of an ending question.

4. Read your riddle to others and see if they guess the answer.

Dual Bio Poems

My name _____ The character _____

Book _____ Date _____

	Myself	**Character**
Name	_____	_____
Four adjectives	_____	_____
Who feels	_____	_____
	_____	_____
	_____	_____
	_____	_____
Who needs	_____	_____
Who likes	_____	_____
Who would like to	_____	_____
Name	_____	_____

Personal Narrative: Written Reflections

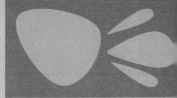

Sometimes writers forget that small moments in life can make wonderful stories. The following visualization experience is designed to assist writers in finding the stories within their own lives that are well worth telling.

Narrowing the Focus

1. Ask students to write down three special memories or things they really enjoy doing.

2. After providing time for quiet reflection, ask each student to tell someone close to them about the three things on their list.

3. Have students mark the one that seemed easiest to talk about.

My Rainy Day Adventure

One rainy afternoon, I got off the bus and raced to the house! It wasn't just raining, it was pouring and I was so cold and wet!

I had forgotten completely about my mom not being home, and that I was supposed to the key to let myself in! I reached the roofed doorway. It was eerie to nobody come to the door. After I'd done everything possible to get attention from someone in the house, Then I remembered the truth, but not the whole truth. I sat down and began to worry and cry at the same time.

With my brain completely unplugged and thinking that I was supposed to go to the Daycare Center, Jan's House I began to walk to Sherwood. I began feel fear as I reached of the hill. The more fear I felt, the more I wanted to the Daycare about a mile from home I began running

Visualizing

1. Guide students through a visualization experience using all of their senses. As you guide their internal reflections, stop often and ask them to write words and phrases or draw pictures that reflect the images rolling through their thoughts. You might make statements such as, "As you imagine yourself in the middle of this special time, what do you see around you? Please write words and phrases that describe what you see."

2. Continue the visualization and list-making process as you direct their thinking to sounds, smells, things to touch, and feelings related to this special something in their lives.

Writing

1. Invite students to begin writing about this special memory or pleasant experience. They might want to use words and phrases from the list they made or to draw images from a picture they drew while going through the visualization.

2. Provide opportunities to share their writing and to talk about the experience.

3. I have students tuck writing experiences such as this into their writing folders or into their writers notebooks.

The goal of this experience is not necessarily a finished piece of writing, but rather a better understanding of how to reach inside and pull out writing that is rich with descriptors and feelings—a retell in the most personal sense.

Student's Written Retell (Fiction)

Writer _____

	Retell #1	**Retell #2**	**Retell #3**
Date	_____	_____	_____
Text	_____	_____	_____
	Score (1–5)	**Score (1–5)**	**Score (1–5)**
Setting	_____	_____	_____
Characters	_____	_____	_____
Complete sequence of events	_____	_____	_____
Problem/ Resolution	_____	_____	_____
Relationship to world knowledge	_____	_____	_____
Opinions	_____	_____	_____
Overall retell	_____	_____	_____

Written Retell (Fiction)

Student Name _____ Date _____

Book Title _____

Author_____

This assessment completed by: Reviewer_____

☐ the author of this retell
☐ peer reviewers
☐ the teacher
☐ the author's parent

	Very detailed		Some details		Not clear
Logical sequence	5	4	3	2	1
Characters	5	4	3	2	1
Character development	5	4	3	2	1
Setting	5	4	3	2	1
The problem	5	4	3	2	1
The resolution	5	4	3	2	1
References to the literary devices used by the author	5	4	3	2	1

Collaborative Grading Format

Title of writing_____ Date _____

Author_____

Student Rating: Circle the number that best describes your opinion.

This piece of writing is:

		Needs improvement			**Excellent**	

1. Interesting to a reader   1   2   3   4   5

Justification:

2. Descriptive, creating clear   1   2   3   4   5
pictures in the mind of
the reader

Justification:

3. Carefully edited for   1   2   3   4   5
punctuation and spelling

Justification:

While working on this writing, I learned _____

_____

I deserve the grade of _____ because _____

_____

Collaborative Grading Format

Title of writing _____ Date _____

Author_____

Teacher Rating: Circle the number that best describes your opinion.

This piece of writing is:

		Needs improvement			**Excellent**	
1.	Interesting to a reader	1	2	3	4	5
	Justification:					
2.	Descriptive, creating clear pictures in the mind of the reader	1	2	3	4	5
	Justification:					
3.	Carefully edited for punctuation and spelling	1	2	3	4	5
	Justification:					

In this piece of writing, I noticed improvement on _____

_____

I believe you deserve the grade of _____ because _____

_____

Informational Summary

Writer _____

Topic _____ Date _____

6   The summary covered all main ideas and included an array of supporting details.

The text was referenced in the summary. On page ____ , it stated that

_____ .

The text features were referenced, in the photo on page ____ , it said

_____ .

Beyond the text, extensions were offered that included logical conclusions, inferences, and ongoing questions on the topic.

---

4   The summary covered most main ideas and many supporting details.

Either the text or text features were referenced, but not both.

The summary had few extensions beyond the text such as logical conclusions, inferences, and ongoing questions.

---

2   The summary covered details but not main ideas.

Facts were accurate.

There was no reference to the text or text features.

There were no text extensions.

---

1   The summary had inaccuracies. Information was minimal.

Writing at Home

Dear Parent(s),

When children write, they learn a lot about reading. They see how words go together and they develop a better understanding of how to communicate.

The writing activity that follows is designed to help children of all ages improve their ability to write descriptively. It can be done with favorite foods you already have in your kitchen, and it should be fun for everyone!

1. Help your child to select one favorite food item from your kitchen. This might be a marshmallow, a chocolate kiss, a scoop of ice cream, a piece of fruit, a cookie, a breakfast cereal, or something else.

2. Explain to your child that you are going to use all of your senses to experience this special food (sight, hearing, smell, touch, taste).

3. Using your eyes: Hold the food item up and really look closely at it. Help your child to describe in detail what he or she sees. Are there wrinkles? Is it smooth? Is there color? As you and your child describe the item, work together to write all of the descriptive words you are using.

4. Use each of the other senses to continue this descriptive process. Are there any sounds associated with this food? Any smells? When you touch it, what does it feel like? When you taste it slowly, what textures and tastes come to mind?

5. Assist your child in reading the list of words you have created about this food experience.

6. We will have a special bulletin board at school waiting to showcase these food explorations. Please have your child draw a picture and then write about this food experience. As your child writes, encourage the use of descriptive words and phrases from the list you created together.

Enjoy!

Plan a Story, Write a Story, Make a Book

Please work with your child to use the three circles on this page to plan a story about your family. It can be something that really happened or a story you make up.

Draw a picture in each circle. These will be the illustrations for your story. Encourage your child to talk a lot about the pictures.

Cut out the circles with your pictures inside and glue them onto three blank pages.

Put the pages in order. Write a story to match the pictures on each page.

Add a front and back cover, plus a title. Staple it together and sign your names. Enjoy reading the book to your family and friends!

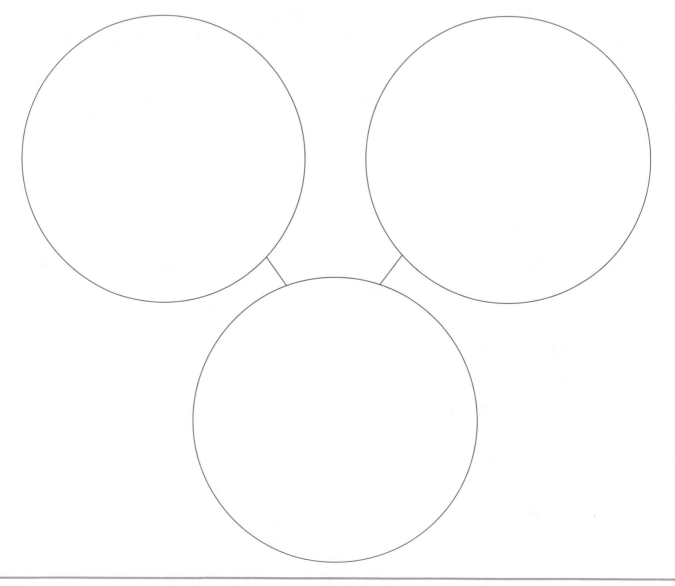

Drawing to Learn

Dear Parents,

You have been watching your children draw since they were very small. Did you know that drawing is very essential to children's understanding of the world? It helps them organize their thinking and satisfies a need for personal response to the world.

The next time you read to your child, you might think about asking your child to draw a picture about the story you read. It would be even better if you drew a picture, too, and then you and your child could talk about your drawings.

When children draw a picture about a story, they have to think about all of the important parts of a story, then choose the part that seems most interesting. While this may sound simple, it is the essence of reading comprehension—the ability to look at all of the information and pick out the important parts.

When children draw and write about a story or an experience, they learn even more. So, please keep reading and drawing!

Your child's teacher

CHAPTER 5 AT-A-GLANCE

Retelling Strategy	Comprehension Strands	Classification of Thinking	Page
Word Prediction	Infer, Question	Generating	172
Read, Cover, Remember, Retell	Summarize	Knowing	174
	Determine importance	Integrating	
Coding Strategy	Activate prior knowledge	Knowing	176
	Connect	Organizing	
	Question	Analyzing	
Weave a Web of Understanding	Summarize	Knowing	178
	Determine importance	Generating	
Student-Created Dictionaries	Synthesize	Organizing	179
	Summarize	Integrating	
Information Equation	Infer	Integrating	180
	Synthesize	Analyzing	
Questioning	Question	Knowing, Analyzing	182
Fact or Fib?	Question	Evaluating	184
	Activate prior knowledge	Integrating	
Test-Style Questions	Question	Knowing, Integrating, Evaluating	186
Magic Jigsaw: A Questioning Strategy	Question	Generating, Applying	188
Focusing on Important Ideas	Determine importance	Analyzing	190
	Summarize	Applying	
Sum It Up	Determine importance	Knowing	191
	Summarize	Organizing	
Reflecting on Main Ideas	Determine importance	Knowing	192
	Synthesize	Organizing	
Nonfiction Scaffold	Summarize	Integrating, Organizing	193
Drawing Conclusions	Synthesize	Integrating	194
	Infer	Generating	
Generalization Strategy	Determine importance	Evaluating	195
	Infer	Generating	
Leads, Middles, Endings!	Synthesize	Evaluating	196
Preparing an Informational Retell	Determine importance	Evaluating	197
	Summarize	Applying	
Table of Contents Retell	Question	Knowing	198
	Summarize	Integrating	
Retelling Expository Text	Summarize	Integrating	199
Book Evaluation	Synthesize	Evaluating	200
Investigating Visual Supports	Synthesize	Evaluating	201
	Use sensory imaging	Analyzing	
Reciprocal Teaching	Question	Knowing	202
	Summarize	Generating	
Alpha Antics	Synthesize	Integrating, Applying	204
Alliteration Fun	Use sensory imaging	Analyzing	206
A Definition Poem	Use sensory imaging	Generating	208
	Determine importance	Integrating	
Research Plan	Summarize	Organizing	209
	Synthesize	Applying	
Investigations	Determine importance	Organizing	210
	Synthesize	Integrating	

Informational Text

Informational text permeates our everyday lives. Newspapers, computer manuals, television directories, maps, cookbooks, and magazines are firmly woven into the texture of our culture. Yet these are the very texts that learners tell us are the most challenging to them.

To become reflective readers and writers of informational text, readers must have both extensive and intensive experience with information-bearing text. They need to be read to from this genre to deepen their understanding of the language structures of expository material. They need to learn to absorb cues from visual supports such as photographs, charts, diagrams, and boldfaced texts (Hoyt 2003). They need to learn how to activate and utilize their own prior knowledge on the topic and to apply a wide range of metacognitive strategies for making meaning while seeking information.

As we reflect on children as readers of informational text, it becomes apparent that we must aggressively engage them at the earliest stages of literacy development

Informational texts invite learners to investigate the real world.

with nonfiction reading. When children read about spiders or ants or magnets, curiosity is stimulated and language flows easily. Informational texts that are predictable and well written provide emergent as well as developing and fluent readers with opportunities to apply their fledgling understandings about print while expanding their world knowledge. They continue to grow

Students need experiences in writing the full array of nonfiction text types.

as readers and writers and deepen their understanding of a genre that will dominate their learning careers.

Using informational text is particularly helpful to children who are learning English as a second language. The concrete nature of the real world makes it easier for these children to create bridges between their first and second languages. They can see direct linguistic matches when objects or animals are the focus of language learning. A worm is a worm, conceptually, in any language. In narrative text, the challenges are much more complex. Cultural issues and complex concepts such as love and emotion are much more difficult to explain to a language learner. It becomes even more difficult when English language learners are fed a steady diet of narrative texts that feature pigs in skirts and other phenomenon that do not exist in their native culture.

To assist learners in becoming reflective and strategic readers of informational text, it is helpful to remember that reading strategies can be taught in all texts. A science teacher, for example, while teaching about gravity might also utilize the text to support metacognitive strategies such as activating prior knowledge and summarizing. These strategies, often thought of as the domain of reading/language arts teaching, will actually assist the science teacher to reach the goal of helping students understand gravity.

For the sake of our students, we must remember that "reading informational text is about concepts and understandings. The more we build upon and connect to prior knowledge, the more the reader will understand and retain. It is also of significant concern that expository *reading* for many students is often a listening experience. Well-meaning teachers, concerned about textbooks that are too difficult, often create situations in which one student reads from the text and others

Informational texts should be subjected to critical/analytical thinking, to ensure reading is deep.

listen or attempt to follow along in the book. This situation does little to build conceptual understandings and can actually deter from the learning process as the "listeners" are engaging in very little reading.

The importance of being able to read and write informational texts critically and well cannot be overstated (Duke 2005). To ensure that we guide our students to the highest possible levels of proficiency with informational sources, I believe we must:

- Provide explicit instruction and think-alouds to show students how to employ comprehension strategies in nonfiction.

Provide explicit instruction and modeling of strategies for navigating informational sources.

- Guide students in building an arsenal of meaning-seeking strategies that will help them understand and retain information.

- Model nonfiction writing every day so students see the wide variety of ways in which writers take notes, record important ideas, write summaries, draft letters to share the content being learned, and write procedural texts and reports.

Model writing and thinking aloud about how a writer of nonfiction marries meaning and craft.

- Rethink schedules to increase the amount of time students spend actually reading and writing in a wide range of informational genre.

- Focus on the concepts in informational texts, helping students to reach deeply as thinkers.

- Make it clear that every text has an author and that author has a point of view. Informational texts must be read critically to consider bias, quality of information, and the craft with which the author presents the content.

- Conduct discussions around informational sources, comparing and contrasting multiple selections on the same topic, considering main ideas, themes, and quality of the writing.

Encourage deep conversations about informational selections, focusing on author point of view, comparison of multiple sources on the same topic, and craft of nonfiction writing.

- Look closely at the balance between fiction and nonfiction to ensure that read-alouds, shared reading, small-group instruction, and independent reading never fall below a 50–50 balance.

- Make a commitment to help students learn to love informational texts. Give them the gift of informational strategies, and activate their innate sense of wonder about the world in which we live.

Build a sense of passion for informational literacy and cultivate a sense of wonder.

Good Readers of Informational Text

* Have clear goals for their reading
* Look over the text before reading, notice illustrations, headings, charts, etc.
* Activate prior knowledge
* Make predictions
* Use meaning and expect the text to make sense
* Understand whether comprehension is occurring
* Make connections: text to self, text to text, text to world
* Create visual images
* Consciously use text features (pictures, headings, captions, boldface type)
* Draw inferences, conclusions
* Ask questions as they read
* Read different kinds of informational texts differently
* Skim and scan to recheck information
* Locate information
* Adjust reading rate to match the demands of the text
* Make a plan when reading informational texts
* Identify important ideas and words
* Consciously shift strategies to match purpose
* Retell, summarize, synthesize
* Use a variety of fix-up strategies
    * ✓ Read on
    * ✓ Backtrack
    * ✓ Context clues
    * ✓ Make substitutions
    * ✓ Look at word parts; beginnings, endings, chunks

Reading Informational Texts

Reader _____ Date _____

As a reader of informational texts, I am learning that _____

_____

When I am getting ready to read, I take time to _____

_____

During reading I know it is important to _____

_____

If I get stuck on a word, I _____

_____

Strategies I am using a lot in informational reading _____

_____

When I am finished reading, I _____

_____

A goal for my next informational book is to _____

_____

Informational books are different from stories because _____

_____

_____

_____

Word Prediction

When students engage in Word Prediction before reading, they activate prior knowledge about the topic and pull forward the academic vocabulary that will assist them in navigating the passage.

I like to model this strategy first as a read-aloud using an enlarged text or a book with pictures that are large enough for all to see. Using the selected text, I model how to preview a text by skimming and scanning pictures, headings, and other graphic supports. Then, I think aloud: "What *words* should I expect to encounter in this passage?" As I think of words that I would expect in a passage on this content, I list the words on a chart so they are visible to all. Finally, I begin reading the selection. Every time one of my predicted words appears in the text, I place a tally next to it. This keeps everyone's attention on the academic vocabulary. Motivating is high as students listen carefully to see which of the words actually appear. Finally, I think aloud about any words that didn't appear, considering why they might not have been selected for this passage. I also think aloud about words I wish I had selected, words that appeared often and were central to the meaning.

With this modeling as a frame, partners and individuals are ready to engage in word predictions on their own.

Word Prediction

Comprehension Strands	Level of Thinking	Action Vocabulary
Infer	Generating	Predict, elaborate, infer
Question		

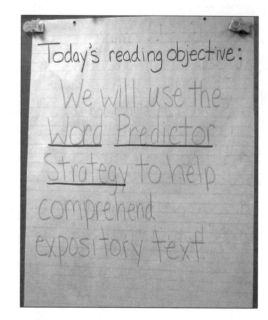

Word predictions activate prior knowledge and stimulate intrinsic motivation.

Word Predictions

Reader(s) _____

Focus topic _____

✱ Before reading:
Preview the text quickly by looking at pictures and other graphic supports. Then *close your book* and work with a partner or a team to list all of the words you think you will encounter in a reading passage about this topic. With each word, tell WHY you think it will appear.

Our words:

<table>
<tr><td></td><td>(✓) appeared during the reading</td></tr>
<tr><td>_____</td><td>_____</td></tr>
<tr><td>_____</td><td>_____</td></tr>
<tr><td>_____</td><td>_____</td></tr>
<tr><td>_____</td><td>_____</td></tr>
<tr><td>_____</td><td>_____</td></tr>
<tr><td>_____</td><td>_____</td></tr>
</table>

✱ During reading:
Watch for your words to see if they appear in the text. Tally each time you find one.

✱ After reading:
Talk to your partners about WHY some words did not appear in the reading selection. What words do you wish you had predicted?

Read, Cover, Remember, Retell

Read, Cover, Remember, Retell is designed to help readers of an informational text to slow down and read for meaning. They begin by reading a fairly small amount of text, then covering the print with their hand. While their hands are over the page, readers take a moment to wonder, "What did I learn?" "What is important?" "What key words and ideas should I remember?" Students quickly learn that if they are unsure and need to recheck the content, they follow the strategy used by good readers and reread the section to give themselves another chance to absorb the content. This pause in reading, followed by self-questioning, generates a midstream retell and solidifies content understanding. The deliberate steps form a routine in which pausing, thinking, self-questioning, and summarizing become naturally integrated into informational reading.

Read, Cover, Remember, Retell

Comprehension Strands	Level of Thinking	Action Vocabulary
Summarize	Knowing	Name, store for recall
Determine importance	Integrating	Connect and combine, summarize

Read, Cover, Remember, Retell scaffolds understanding as partners read and reflect on short passages.

Read, Cover, Remember, Retell also scaffolds independent reading.

When students are first using the strategy, I have them work with a partner so the retell step has an authentic audience. As readers gain sophistication with the strategy, they can do an internal retell before reading on.

In all cases, they should never read more than they think they can cover with their hand when the topic is new and they are striving to hold on to the content.

Kelly Marks at Wingate Elementary keeps mini-strategy posters in a small spiral binder she uses when conferring with readers.

The Steps:

Read

First, read a small amount of text.

Cover

Cover the text with your hand.

Remember

Think about the meaning. Remember what is under your hand.

Retell

Tell a partner what you remember. If you aren't sure, go back and "sneak a peek!"

(Demonstrated by Carolyn from Howard County, Maryland. Photos by Kelly Davis)

Read, Cover, Remember, Retell Bookmarks

Cut these out and use with your books.

Read only as much as your hand can cover.

Cover the words with your hand.

Remember what you have just read. (It is OK to take another look.)

Retell what you just read inside your head or to a partner.

Read

Cover

Remember

Retell

Read

Cover

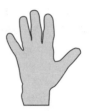

Remember

REREAD! (Think about *why* you are rereading.)

Coding Strategy

This strategy is designed to help students be reflective readers, pausing and weighing what they are reading against their prior knowledge. It also increases the likelihood that students will engage in self-questioning as they read.

Because students need to write their reactions next to what they are reading, it works best to have them read from photocopies. An alternative that saves paper is to have students paper clip one-inch-wide strips of paper down the margin of each page they read or place sticky notes down the side, and then place their "codes" on these pieces of paper.

As students read, their task is to stop at each sentence or each paragraph and indicate their reactions to their reading in the following ways.

* **I already knew this!**

+ **New information**

! **Wow**

?? **I don't understand**

Coding Strategy

Comprehension Strands	Level of Thinking	Action Vocabulary
Activate prior knowledge	Knowing	Formulate questions, label
Connect	Organizing	Categorize
Question	Analyzing	Analyze, differentiate

I find it helpful to begin by having students work with a photocopy or lay a piece of transparency film over the page. This enables them to place their "codes" right on the text. Then, they meet with partners, compare their coding, and move onto the next page.

As students gain sophistication with this strategy, they can record their codes on two-inch-wide strips of paper that they paper clip to the margin of the page.

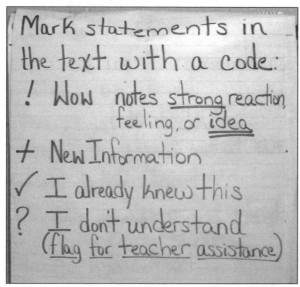

Clearly labeled posters help students keep the codes in mind as they read.

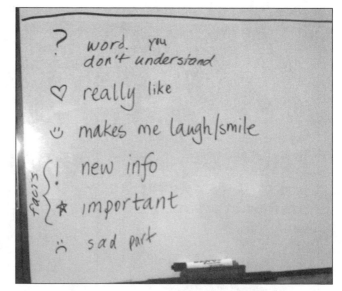

You may want to personalize codes for you and your students.

Coding Strategy

Name of reader _____ Title of text _____

Date _____

KEY:

    ✱   **I already knew this!**

    +   **New information**

    !   **Wow**

    ??   **I don't understand**

After coding a section of your text, meet with a partner to share and compare the codes you each have marked. Share your thinking and tell why you coded the sections as you did.

How did this strategy help you as a reader? _____

_____

Record the most important ideas from your reading here.

Weave a Web of Understanding

After taking time to reflect on a topic or an informational text, students gather in a circle. The first student holds a ball of yarn and tells one thing that is remembered about the focus text. While the first student holds onto the end of the string, the ball of yarn is passed across, not around, the circle to another student. This student tells one more thing that is remembered and holds onto the string while passing the ball across the circle to another student. As the ball of yarn continues to be passed, it forms a "web."

If the ball gets to a student who cannot think of a reflection that hasn't already been stated, it is acceptable to repeat an idea.

Weave a Web of Understanding		
Comprehension Strands	**Level of Thinking**	**Action Vocabulary**
Summarize	Knowing	List, name, recall, identify
Determine importance	Generating	Explain, add details

Weave a Web levels the playing field so all team members have opportunities to contribute ideas.

This strategy works both in a whole class and in small-group formats, but intensity for individual learners is greater in a small group. The strategy provides a forum in which all students understand they must take responsibility to contribute ideas—as the ball of yarn moves around the group, quieter students anticipate and prepare while more verbal students learn the art of patience as they must wait for their turn to talk.

This is an interactive language-building strategy that works across all dimensions of the curriculum.

Weave a Web can be done with a larger group but this format reduces participation and increases the time students spend waiting to contribute their thinking.

Student-Created Dictionaries

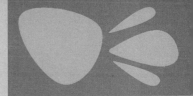

Dictionaries are a wonderful structure that invite students to revisit recent topics or favorite literature selections while developing a deeper understanding of a genre (dictionaries) they will use throughout life. To create a dictionary, students make lists of all the words they can think of that relate to a certain topic. They then write definitions for each of the words on half sheets of paper. (Be sure to have them revise for content and edit for conventions.) The next step is to put the definitions in alphabetical order and decide how many words will go on each page, as well as which ones should be illustrated. The last step is to insert guide words at the top of each page. More proficient readers and writers might even want to divide their words into syllables!

Dictionaries

Comprehension Strands	Level of Thinking	Action Vocabulary
Synthesize	Organizing	Change the form but not the substance
Summarize	Integrating	Connect and combine, generalize

On a topic

The Soccer Dictionary

FIELD   GOAL

Field. A grass area where you play soccer

Flags. When the ball has gone out of bounds, the flag is raised.

Forward. A person who waits at center field then dribbles the ball up to the goal.

Goal. The place you kick the ball.

Reflecting on a book

Faithful Elephants

A Thoughtful Dictionary

SNAKES   SYRINGE

Snakes. The snakes died quickly. They did not suffer.

Stop. The zookeepers wanted the war to stop.

Survive. The elephants tried not to die.

Syringe. A needle used for injections.

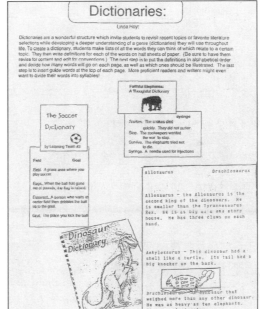

Student-created dictionaries provide powerful content review while helping students understand the structure of a dictionary.

Dictionary construction requires alphabetizing, use of guide words, concise summaries, and use of academic vocabulary.

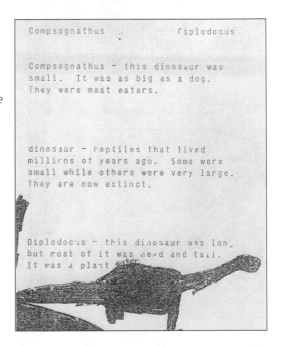

Information Equation

Information equations are designed to help students notice and clarify relationships between ideas and concepts. Using a mathematical format, students generate equations to show relationships and dependencies between elements of the natural world.

Inferences, cause and effect, and relationships lift student thinking to higher levels when they create Information Equations.

Some examples:

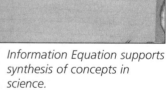

Information Equation

Comprehension Strands	Level of Thinking	Action Vocabulary
Infer	Integrating	Connect, combine, restructure
Synthesize	Analyzing	Examine relationships

Spider + web + fly = spider dinner

Seed + soil + water + sun = growing seedling

Hibernating frog + warming air = springtime wake-up call

The Deer Family

fast runner + high jumper = escape

hiding in shadows + danger = escape trying t

white spots + tall grass = hidden

skinny legs + long muscles = run fast

Emergent readers can do the thinking while the teacher records their equations.

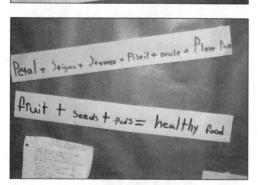

Petal + Stigma + Stamen + Pistil + ovule = Plant Par

fruit + seeds + pods = healthy food

Sentence strips encourage students to create longer, more complex equations.

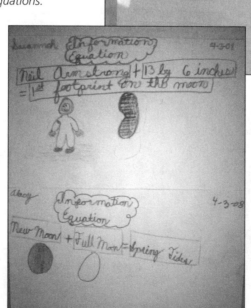

Science Information Equations

• crystals + water droplets = rain
• dust + water = cloud
• rain particles + Cumulus Cloud = Nimbo Cumulus Cloud
• cumulonimbus clouds + in the sky = thunderstorm
• Stratus + Cumulus = stormy

Information Equation supports synthesis of concepts in science.

A study of space uses Information Equation to integrate social studies and science concepts.

Information Equation

Name of Student _____ Topic _____ Date _____

Information Equation:

_____ + _____ = _____

This is important because _____

Information Equation:

_____ + _____ = _____

This is important because _____

Information Equation:

_____ + _____ = _____

This is important because _____

Questioning

One of our key objectives as comprehension coaches is to get our students to challenge the texts they read with the same level of intensity they apply to understanding a video game or the hinges in the jaw of a venomous snake. We need to encourage and celebrate questions about a text, about a topic, about validity of the content, about relevance to our world, comparisons to other texts on the topic, and so on.

Questioning

Comprehension Strand	Level of Thinking	Action Vocabulary
Question	Knowing	Formulate questions, clarify information
	Analyzing	Examine relationships, main ideas

Questions, when encouraged and supported, build motivation and increase engagement.

Partners challenge each other with questions about the text, about the craft of the author, and about their understanding of the print.

In developing a classroom culture in which questions thrive, I frequently think aloud in front of students about the difference between surface questions, those with a right/wrong answer, and deep questions that cause us to think beyond the text making connections, inferences, and synthesizing knowledge. My goal is to make it clear to students that some kinds of questions are designed just to check our existing knowledge, while others are designed to help us reach deeper and understand more fully.

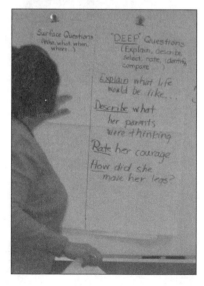

Modeling the creation of surface vs. deep questions sets the stage for improved comprehension.

Question-Generating Strategy

1. Preview a text.
   Read titles, subheadings, and the table of contents
   Look at pictures or illustrations.
   Read the *first paragraph.*

2. Think of an "I wonder" question. Write it down.

   I wonder _____

   _____

3. Read the text to answer your question. Write the answer when you find it.

   _____

   _____

   _____

4. Ask yourself another "I Wonder" question, then read the next section to find the answer.

   I wonder _____

   _____

5. Continue to read small segments—be sure to ask your self a question *before* each section.

6. Write or draw to show the most important ideas you learned.

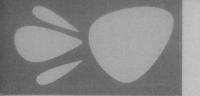

Fact or Fib?

This strategy is fun, a stretch for understanding, and a great way for students to celebrate the efforts of their peers! Students utilize this strategy to reflect upon a unit of study, a favorite literature selection, or a current event.

1. Have them make a list of facts that they remember from the text.

2. For each fact, they need to decide if they will write the answer as a fact or a fib. For example:

   Statement: "Bat wings have skin on them." Fact or Fib?
   Answer: "Fact. They have thin, flexible skin, not feathers."

3. The students enjoy folding 5 x 7 cards in half, writing their statement on the front and their answers inside.

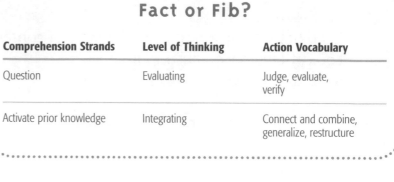

Fact or Fib?

Comprehension Strands	Level of Thinking	Action Vocabulary
Question	Evaluating	Judge, evaluate, verify
Activate prior knowledge	Integrating	Connect and combine, generalize, restructure

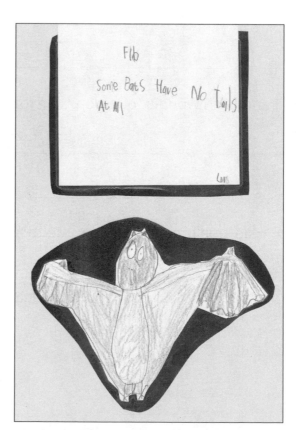

In Fact or Fib, writers create a statement on the front of a flap covering the answer.

The flap is lifted to expose the answer to a partner.

Fact or Fib? Thanks to Jodi Wolson, instructional coach, Spokane, Washington.

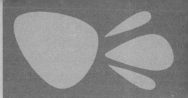

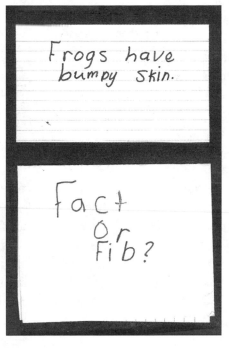

Frogs have bumpy skin.

Fact or Fib?

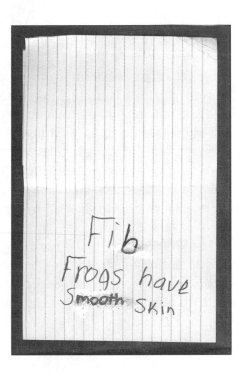

Fib Frogs have smooth skin

Cheetahs have heart-shaped dots.

Fact or Fib?

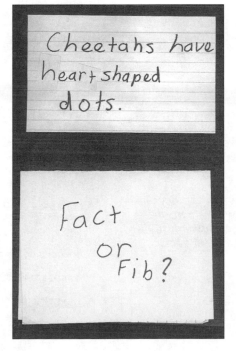

Fib Cheetahs have egged shaped dots.

Test-Style Questions

Standardized tests, whether we like them or not, are a type of text that our students must learn to navigate. Rather than passing out reams of test practice materials with little relevance to core curriculum, I have students create Test-Style Questions as a structure for reviewing units of study in science, social studies, mathematics, and so on. This keeps them focused on reviewing the core content, while helping students become familiar with the genre of "test."

I begin by modeling and explaining how a test writer constructs a question. My goal is to help the students understand that once the question is drafted, the writer needs to insert one correct answer and three distractors that are almost correct.

Test-Style Questions

Comprehension Strand	Level of Thinking	Action Vocabulary
Question	Knowing	Formulate questions
	Integrating	Generalize, restructure
	Evaluating	Evaluate, judge

To scaffold appropriate language for the test-style questions, I provide students with a selection of test stems to help them launch the questions using the formal register of standardized assessment. This list will get you started, but you may want to identify those stems that most commonly occur in your own state or refer to page 367 in *Spotlight on Comprehension* (Hoyt 2005) for a more complete list.

Model the thinking behind a Test-Style Question, using the formal language patterns often found in a standardized measure.

Example

There is enough information to suggest that _____

Which sentence best tells ...

All of these are true except _____

According to this selection _____

Why did _____ happen?

The passage was mostly about

Show students how a test writer inserts the correct answer first, then adds the "distractors."

Example

The main purpose of this is _____

A main idea could be identified as _____

In the selection, _____ means _____

What conclusion can you draw?

Which statement is not true?

A good title for this selection would be _____

What did _____ probably mean?

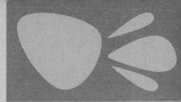

Once students catch on to the format, we shift to shared writing of questions on a variety of topics. When they're ready, partners and individuals craft Test-Style Questions of their own. Students love to exchange questions, trying to stump each other.

Once students understand the format for Test-Style Questions, they work in teams to create their own.

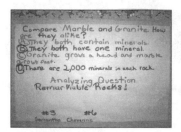

A study of geology is enhanced with Test-Style Questions for content review.

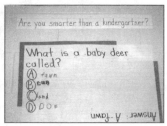

Even kindergartners can have fun playing with the genre of test while reviewing informational content.

Being Strategic

A vital element of this study of test as a genre is to model the thinking that supports a good test taker. Using the questions generated by partners or teams of students, think out loud about how you narrow your options, eliminate obviously incorrect answers, reread a passage to check yourself, and so on. Help the students develop a sensitivity to navigating the questions in a strategic way by ensuring that they hear you think aloud as a problem solver.

I further this focus by asking students to explain their thinking when they trade questions with others. I remind them that it isn't enough to get the answer right. We need to know how we came up with the answer and to be clear about the processes we used to navigate the "test."

Beat the Teacher

Students especially love it when we shift to Beat the Teacher and the teacher has to attempt to answer the questions students have created. For Beat the Teacher, students work independently or with partners to create poster-size versions of a Test-Style Question related to a unit of study. Then, the teacher takes the hot seat while students attempt to "Beat the Teacher" with stellar Test-Style Questions.

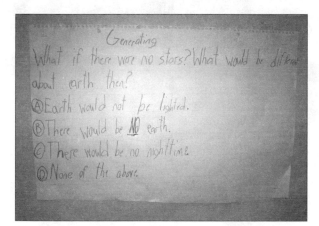

With practice, students learn to tune their Test-Style Questions to match Marzano's Classifications of Thinking.

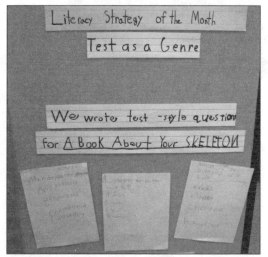

Test is a genre worthy of investigation, especially when it can be linked to core academic curriculum.

Magic Jigsaw: A Questioning Strategy

A very special educator by the name of Caroline Papulski took an origami class and then quickly realized that the fascinating folded shape presented in class was a perfect vehicle for collecting student-generated questions.

Students have a wonderful time designing questions and answers that they can share with one another.

The following template profiles the steps in constructing a Magic Jigsaw that can be used:

✱ as a post-reading summary, to showcase questions.

✱ before reading, to profile questions that guide research.

✱ during reading, to collect questions that remain unanswered and need further research.

The steps are as shown on the following page.

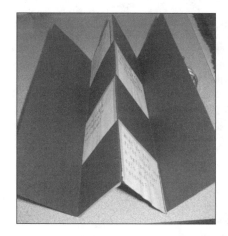

It is essential to fold the jigsaw into a W before attempting to expose the the answers hiding in the interior spaces.

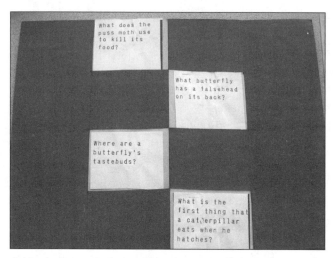

A Magic Jigsaw is designed to showcase student-generated questions.

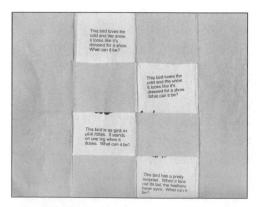

Materials List:

Option 1:
8″ × 11″ photocopy weight paper (1 per student)
strips of tag board cut to 2.75″ × 8″ (2 per student)

Option 2:
9″ × 12″ colored construction paper (1 per student)
Strips of tag board cut to 3″ × 9″ (2 per student)

1. Hold the paper vertically, then fold it in half with a horizontal fold (hamburger fold)

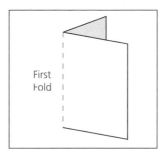

2. Fold the paper one more time, creating a second fold that is parallel to the first.

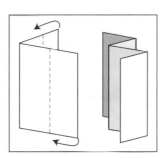

3. Cut or tear from the center fold to the second fold to create four tabs.

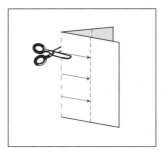

4. Weave strips of colored, tag weight paper into the large sheet, creating a checkerboard.

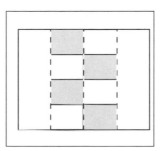

5. Place student-generated questions on the colored squares.

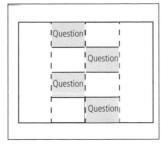

6. Lay the paper sheet on a table top and fold it so it looks like the letter *w* when you look down the end.

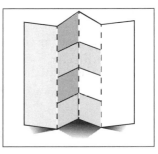

7. At the center peak of the *w*, place your thumbs between the strips of colored paper, sliding them down into the fold.

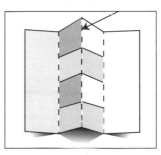

8. Rolling your thumbs away from each other, open the space between the two colored strips. The shape will now be much smaller, with blank squares exposed. This is where you write the answers.

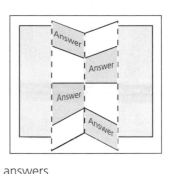

9. Pull on the outside edges of the sheet to return the Magic Jigsaw to its large-size format and expose the questions again.

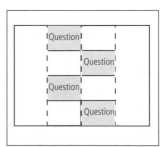

Focusing on Important Ideas

Reader _____ Text _____

1. Skim headings, charts, and paragraph openings. What does most of the information seem to be about?

_____

_____

2. If there are questions at the end of the chapter, skim them. What are some key points to watch for while reading?

_____

_____

3. What are some questions of your own on this topic?

_____

_____

4. Pick a "during reading" strategy such as Coding or VIP to help you get the most from the text.

5. While reading, stop often to think about what you are reading. You might want to look for a summary at the end of each section to help you focus on key ideas.

6. Remember: The goal is to pick the most important information.

7. After reading, stop and think about what you learned.

8. Look at your personal questions. Were they answered? _____

9. Talk to someone about what you learned. You might also want to write, draw, or make a list of key ideas to remember.

10. Think about how you helped yourself be a good reader. What did you do that helped you focus on meaning while reading?

_____

Sum It Up

Reader _____ Text _____ Date _____

Good readers take time to stop reading and think about what they have learned. As you read today, stop at the end of each page and think. What did I just learn? What is most important?

Page # _____   Sum It Up Notes

_____

_____

Page # _____   Sum It Up Notes

_____

_____

Page # _____   Sum It Up Notes

_____

_____

Page # _____   Sum It Up Notes

_____

_____

Page # _____   Sum It Up Notes

_____

_____

When you have finished reading, review your notes. If you were to tell someone what you learned, what would you say?

_____

_____

_____

Reflecting on Main Ideas

Use this chart to retell the key points for a partner or your family.

Name _____ Date _____

Book _____

Page Number	Main Idea (Select one)	Most Important Details (Choose one or two)

Nonfiction Scaffold

Name _____ Date _____

Topic/Book _____

Before I read I thought _____

_____

After reading more I found _____

_____

Besides this, I learned _____

_____

Finally, I noticed that _____

_____

Create an illustration to show something you learned from your investigation.

Drawing Conclusions

When readers draw conclusions from their reading, it is much easier to make generalizations and determine important ideas.

Reader _____   Text _____

Topic _____   Date _____

Facts from my reading:

_____

_____

_____

_____

Conclusions I can draw include:

_____

_____

_____

_____

I believe the very most important ideas are:

_____

_____

_____

Generalization Strategy

Name _____ Date _____

Resources used _____

Student Challenge: Identify the three *most important ideas* in the passage or in your unit of study. Justify your opinions with page numbers, specific points in a text, or with points you have gathered from several sources. The important point is WHY you think these ideas are *more important* than others.

Essential Understanding 1: Draw and/or write

Justification:_____

_____

Essential Understanding 2: Draw and/or write

Justification:_____

_____

Essential Understanding 3: Draw and/or write

Justification:_____

_____

Leads, Middles, Endings!

Create a classroom resource of powerful information leads, strong middles that keep you going, and endings that summarize. You might develop this as a bulletin board with quotes collected from great informational books, as a big book, or in personal logs the students refer to independently.

Encourage the students to include student-authored texts as well as published works in this survey.

Then ... write:

What makes a good lead? _____

_____

_____

_____

What keeps a reader going in the middle of an informational text?_____

_____

_____

_____

_____

What are the attributes of a great ending?_____

_____

_____

_____

Preparing an Informational Retell

Reader _____ Title of book _____

Topic _____ Date _____

Prepare a retell of the important points in this book. Select several of the boxes below that will help you remember the key ideas. (You don't need to use all of the boxes.) In each of the boxes you select, you can choose to either draw a quick sketch or jot down your thinking. The goal is to use this sheet to help yourself prepare to retell the most important information from this reading.

Place a ✓ in the boxes you select.

☐ What was the main idea the author was trying to communicate?

☐ What else did you learn?

☐ If you were to write about this topic and tell just the most important parts, what would you include?

☐ What was the most interesting part of this book?

☐ If you were going to do further research on this topic, what would you want to learn?

☐ Did you think the author presented the information well? Why or why not?

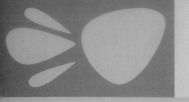

Table of Contents Retell

Select a text and preview the table of contents *before* reading. Have students write questions about each section of the table of contents. Engage the students in searching for answers to their questions by reading the focus text and/or utilizing other resources.

After the reading and researching, ask each student to return to the table of contents and think of at least one thing that was learned regarding each section of the contents page. Move to a paired sharing in which partners tell each other what they learned about each subtopic listed.

This strategy could be advanced to a collaborative effort by labeling sheets of butcher paper with the subheadings from the contents page and then placing them around the room. Partners or cooperative groups could then move around the room adding their personal collections of evidence to each sheet. The final collections could be typed into a student-authored book on the topic.

Example of a student response using Table of Contents Retell:

Table of Contents Retell

Comprehension Strands	Level of Thinking	Action Vocabulary
Question	Knowing	Formulate questions
Summarize	Integrating	Summarize, generalize restructure

Kitchen Science

Table of Contents section	*Before* Reading: Questions generated from the table of contents	*During* Reading: Answers I found while reading	*After* Reading: An important point from this section of the book
The Bouncing Egg	How can an egg bounce? Won't it break?	Minerals in the eggshell make it hard but vinegar can remove the minerals, leaving a soft ball that can bounce if you drop it gently.	Substances can change. When you add a new ingredient like vinegar, the eggshell actually dissolves, leaving a soft "ball" behind.
Dancing Peppercorns	Peppercorns have no muscles. They can't dance.	If you activate static electricity on an inflated balloon, the electricity attracts the pepper and makes it jump around when the balloon is held over the top.	I think of electricity in terms of appliances and light fixtures. It is amazing to think that static electricity can make things move.

Retelling Expository Text

What is the topic?

What are the most important ideas to remember?

What did you learn that you didn't already know?

What is the setting for this information?

What did you notice about the organization and text structure?

What did you notice about the visuals such as the graphs, charts, and pictures?

Can you summarize what you learned?

What do you think was the author's purpose for writing this piece?

Book Evaluation

Name _____ Date _____

Name of Book _____ Author _____

	Great		OK		Not so great
	1	2	3	4	5
The author made the information easy to understand.	1	2	3	4	5
The writing style was comfortable to read.	1	2	3	4	5
The book was organized in a logical way.	1	2	3	4	5
The author explained ideas completely before shifting topics.	1	2	3	4	5
The charts, graphs, pictures, and other visuals were helpful.	1	2	3	4	5
The table of contents and index were organized and easy to use.	1	2	3	4	5
My overall rating of this book:	1	2	3	4	5

Investigating Visual Supports

Review Team _____

Your job is to review at least ten informational books and think carefully about the visuals in the books. How do the visuals help you? Are these examples well chosen? Do the pages look inviting? Do they draw you into the reading? Why? Check for captions and other features we know support reading.

Book Reviewed   **Rating**

1. _____   5   4   3   2   1

Why did you give it this rating? _____

2. _____   5   4   3   2   1

Why did you give it this rating? _____

3. _____   5   4   3   2   1

Why did you give it this rating? _____

4. _____   5   4   3   2   1

Why did you give it this rating? _____

5. _____   5   4   3   2   1

Why did you give it this rating? _____

What did you learn about visuals and your own preferences?

_____

_____

_____

Reciprocal Teaching

Step 1:

Take time to help students learn about the four underpinnings of reciprocal teaching and learning. I read an informational text to the students and stop often throughout the reading to model the following processes, completing all steps for each section.

Reciprocal Teaching

Comprehension Strands	Level of Thinking	Action Vocabulary
Question	Knowing	Clarify information, formulate questions
Summarize	Generating	Predict, explain, elaborate

✱ *Predict.* What do you think the next section is going to be about? What information might be included?

✱ *Clarify.* What did the author mean when he or she said _____? What does the word _____ mean on page _____?

✱ *Ask yourself questions.* What were the important ideas?

✱ *Orally summarize the reading.* State main ideas and important details up to this point in the reading.

Step 2:

After several think-aloud experiences with the process, students are ready to continue the process in small groups. The teacher is a member of the group and takes a turn as group leader, just as the students do. Reading segments are kept short so that the students can work together to negotiate meaning in manageable chunks. The group leader reads the cards shown on page 201, one at a time, and guides the discussion.

The set of cards are passed to the next group member and the process is repeated with the next segment of reading and a new group leader.

Reciprocal Teaching involves peers in clarifying and reaching for deeper levels of under-standing.

Teacher participation in a Reciprocal Teaching group lifts engagement and provides for assessment opportunities.

The teacher is a participant, not a leader, so the students do most of the talking during a reciprocal group.

Adapted from Palinscar and Brown.

Reciprocal Teaching Cards

To use before each section.

Card #1. "Please get ready to read to _____." (Select a boldfaced heading or an apparent stopping point in the text. Have all team members mark the stop point with a sticky note.)	**Card #2.** "Who will make the first prediction?"
Card #3. "Does anyone else have a prediction?" (Encourage group members to speak.)	**Card #4.** "Please read silently to the point we selected."

To use after reading each section.

Card #5. "Are there any words you thought were interesting?" (Invite group members to speak.)	**Card #6.** "Are there any ideas you found interesting or puzzling?" (Invite group members to contribute.)
Card #7. "Do you have comments about the reading?" (Group response.)	**Card #8.** "Who will begin our summary?" "Who can add to that?"

Pass the cards to the new leader.

Alpha Antics

Students reflect on what they have learned about a topic and then begin listing words that reflect their understanding.

For example, while studying about eagles, students might decide that *wingspan, protected status,* and *eyesight* are critical understandings. Using the format on page 203, they might write:

Alpha Antics

Comprehension Strand	Level of Thinking	Action Vocabulary
Synthesize	Integrating	Connect and combine, generalize
	Applying	Demonstrate, apply, use in a new context

Example

Eagle

W is for eagle. *Because they can have up to an eight-foot wingspan.*

P is for eagle. *Because eagles are protected by law.*

E is for eagle. *Because eagles have incredible eyesight and can see much better at a distance than a human.*

Example for snow:

Example

Snow

M is for snowman. *Because eventually all snowmen melt.*

Example for worms:

Example

Worm

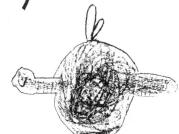

A is for worm.

Why?

Because a worm eats apples.

Alpha Antics

Topic _____

_____ is for _____

Because _____

_____

_____ is for _____

Because _____

_____

_____ is for _____

Because _____

_____

Illustration

Adapted from *Q is for Duck* by Mary Elting and Michael Folsom.

Alliteration Fun

Poetic formats add variety to informational learning. They also stimulate visual images, which can enhance long-term learning and descriptive writing.

The Process

Students write three word clusters that describe a topic. All words must start with the same letter. The clusters then form an informational poem.

Diane Walworth guided first and second graders in writing:

Apples

Crisp, crunchy, crackly apples
Round, red, rotten apples
Smelly, smooth, succulent apples
Apples

Leaves

Lovely, little, light leaves
Beautiful, brown, big leaves
Wet, windy, wonderful leaves
Crunchy, colorful, crooked leaves
Nasty, nice, nutty leaves
Falling, fun, funny leaves
Gliding, good, green leaves
Cracked, crispy, crushed leaves
Pretty piles of pinkish leaves
Leaves, Leaves, Leaves

In Hood River, Oregon, first graders experiencing the joys of freshly picked Hood River apples write:

Apples, Apples, Apples

Crunchy, crispy, curvy, caramel apples.
Mushy, munchy, mucky, monster apples.
Yummy, yucky, yellow, young apples.
Wormy, wonderful, wet, washed apples.
Good, golden, great, green, apples.
Red, rotten, round, ripe apples.
Smooth, smelly, sparkly, shiny apples.
Juicy, giant, junky, jumbo apples.
Hard, holey, handy, humongous apples.
Apples, apples, apples!

—*by Phyliss Coat's first-grade class*

Alliteration Fun

_____
the topic

_____ , _____ , _____ , _____
the topic

_____ , _____ , _____ , _____
the topic

_____ , _____ , _____ , _____
the topic

_____
the topic

A Definition Poem

_____

Name it

_____

Describe it, rename it

_____

Tell where it would be found

_____

Tell more about it

_____

Use emotion words to tell how you feel about this

_____

Explain why you used the emotion words on line 5

Example:
Eagle
Our national bird
Soaring near mountains and trees
King of the air
Awesome predator
Respected and feared by all

Research Plan

Topic _____

Name _____ Date _____

I am very interested in learning more about _____

_____

I already know that _____

_____

_____

To gather more information I will use _____

_____

I will present my information in the form of (oral presentation, display, report, readers theatre script, song, student-authored book, or something else)_____

_____

I expect to be finished by _____

My Action Plan: Steps to Success

First I will _____

Then I will _____

After that I plan to _____

Finally, I will_____

to demonstrate what I have learned.

Investigations

Knowing that we live in an information age where we can no longer expect to master all knowledge, we must recognize that the most important issue is teaching readers and writers how to *find* information when they need it and then how to *present* it in a way that is usable and comprehensible to others.

Investigations are short probes into a topic. The student selects the topic, engages in brief research, and then presents the work both visually and orally.

Investigations

Comprehension Strands	Level of Thinking	Action Vocabulary
Determine importance	Organizing	Represent, group
Synthesize	Integrating	Connect and combine information

A final form needs to have:

* a title

* a diagram or map

* a border related to the topic

* a layout that measures 11" × 17"

* neatly written paragraphs

Example

Investigations help students to synthesize their learning as they use visuals, text features, and well-constructed text to share their learning with others.

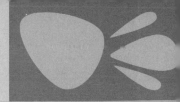

Example

Investigations help students attend to nonfiction conventions. Notice how the illustration spills over the gutter space between the two pages of the layout.

Example

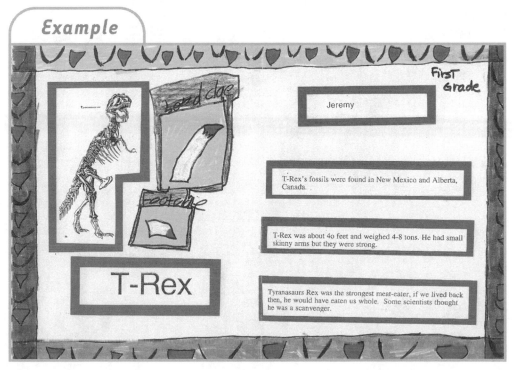

Jeremy's T-Rex Investigation.

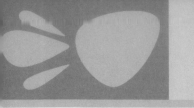
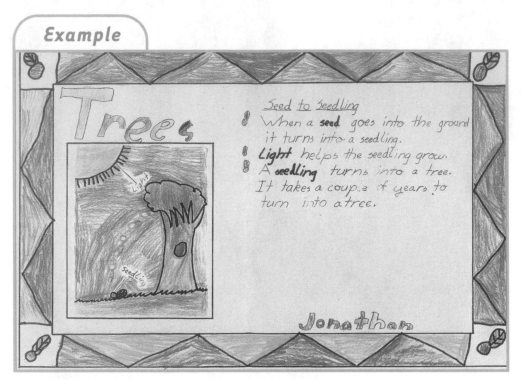

Boldfaced words signal "key words" that were identified during reading.

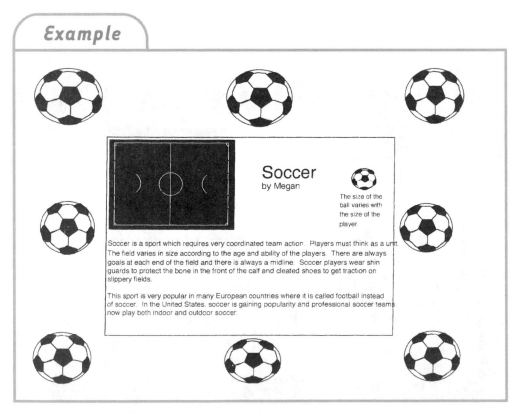

Meagan's Soccer Investigation.

My Investigation

Name _____ Date _____

My Topic _____

Important facts I have learned _____

_____

_____

I will include a map or diagram of _____

My drawings will be _____

My border will be _____

Rough Sketch of Investigation

Informational Retell

Reader_____ Book _____

Data Collected by _____ Topic _____ Date _____

Unassisted Retell

Record in each box with tally marks or anecdotal notes.

   Please tell me about the book you just read. I will be listening for the main ideas as well as for interesting facts you include. I am also interested in what you thought about the book. Please feel free to point to the pictures and any parts of the text that will help you share your learning.

Main Ideas	Details	Use of Text Features

Questioning	Conclusions	Inferences

Connections	Mental Pictures

Assisted Retell

If the information provided above is sketchy, you may want to ask a few probing questions to elicit more from the reader. Try to keep your questions open-ended, such as: Can you tell more about how _____? Were there any other points in the reading you found to be important? If you were going to tell your friend about this, is there anything else you would add? Were you able to make any connections while you were reading?

6   The reader states all main ideas and provides supporting details. Key concepts are understood accurately and extensions may be offered in the form of opinions or connections.

4   The reader is able to state most of the main ideas and provides a range of supporting details. Most concepts are understood accurately.

2   The reader identifies some main ideas and a few supporting details. There may be a few inaccuracies or underdeveloped concepts.

1   The reader is not able to identify the main ideas. Information is incomplete and/or inaccurate.

Observation Guide: Reading of Informational Text

Student _____ Date _____

Assessment completed by _____

		minimal				substantial
1.	As the student previewed the pictures, the information gathered was	1	2	3	4	5

		word by word				smoothly
2.	In a one-on-one conference, the student read the material	1	2	3	4	5

		used only one strategy				used multiple strategies
3.	The student used a variety of strategies for unknown words	1	2	3	4	5

		rarely				most of the time
4.	The reader's miscues maintained meaning	1	2	3	4	5

		rarely				most of the time
5.	The reader self-corrected when meaning broke down	1	2	3	4	5

		rarely				most of the time
6.	The reader cross-checked with grapho-phonic cues	1	2	3	4	5

		inadequate attempt				very complete retell
7.	The reader provided a retell that encompassed key concepts and did not dwell on lesser details	1	2	3	4	5

		has few strategies				describes multiple strategies
8.	The reader described strategies for making meaning in informational text	1	2	3	4	5

Observation Guide: Writing of Informational Text

Student_____ Date_____

Assessment completed by _____

		limited understanding			substantial understanding	
1.	The writing shows understanding of the topic.	1	2	3	4	5
		not organized			well organized	
2.	The writing is organized in a logical way.	1	2	3	4	5
		not visuals			good visuals	
3.	There are visuals to support the written text.	1	2	3	4	5
		little evidence of effort			well laid out	
4.	The layout of the writing and visuals are visually appealing.	1	2	3	4	5
		details only			substantial concepts	
5.	There is an emphasis on key concepts in this writing.	1	2	3	4	5
		too many details			well done	
6.	Details are used to support key concepts and do not dominate the writing.	1	2	3	4	5
		few descriptors			many descriptors	
7.	Descriptions are adequate for a reader to create visual images while reading.	1	2	3	4	5
		needs assistance			well done	
8.	Conventions such as punctuation and spelling have been adequately addressed.	1	2	3	4	5
		limited understanding			right on!	
9.	The writer understands the steps of gathering information, planning, writing, revising, and editing.	1	2	3	4	5
		not present			strongly felt	
10.	The writer's voice is evident in this writing.	1	2	3	4	5

During-Reading Strategy Observation

As you conference with students who are reading expository text, indicate which strategies are being used.

The Reader _____ Date _____

The Book _____

The Reader	Strategy observed	Notes
Uses the table of contents	☐	
Skims through the text before reading	☐	
During reading, pauses to use pictures, graphs, and so on	☐	
Uses the index or glossary if needed	☐	
Uses titles, subheadings, and bold print	☐	
Varies reading rate to match the demands of the text	☐	
Rereads to confirm understanding	☐	
Uses context clues to derive meaning for unknown words	☐	
Substitutes synonyms for unknown words to attempt to maintain meaning	☐	
Self-corrects when meaning breaks down	☐	

Overall rating:

	still needs assistance			very effective use
How effectively did the student uses the above strategies while reading?	1	2	3	4	5

Project Evaluation

Name _____ Date _____

Project _____

Team Members _____

	Student Rating	Teacher Rating
Quality of Ideas Key concepts and conclusions are clearly expressed	1 2 3 4 5	1 2 3 4 5
Expression of Ideas A variety of communication tools are used (writing, illustrations, maps, graphs, models, etc.)	1 2 3 4 5	1 2 3 4 5
Creativity Visually interesting, use of unusual media or forms of communicating	1 2 3 4 5	1 2 3 4 5
Conventions Conventional spelling, punctuation, grammar, effort in editing, looks polished	1 2 3 4 5	1 2 3 4 5
Oral Presentation Organized, audible, clearly explained	1 2 3 4 5	1 2 3 4 5
Participation All members shared in the work	1 2 3 4 5	1 2 3 4 5

Comments: _____

_____

Book Review: Nonfiction

Name _____ Date _____

Title of Book _____ Author _____

What was your opinion of this book?

What did the author do especially well?

What could the author have improved in the book?

What did you learn that was especially interesting?

How did the author use visuals such as graphs, photographs, or charts to explain the topic?

What did you learn about the craft of informational writing?

What techniques can you apply in your own writing?

Informational Book Rating

Name _____ Date _____

Name of Book _____

Author _____ Illustrator _____

		Outstanding		OK		Not so great
1.	The author made the information easy to understand.	5	4	3	2	1
2.	The writing style was comfortable to read.	5	4	3	2	1
3.	The book was organized in a logical way.	5	4	3	2	1
4.	The author explained ideas completely before shifting topics.	5	4	3	2	1
5.	The charts, graphs, and pictures were helpful.	5	4	3	2	1
6.	The table of contents and index were organized and easy to use.	5	4	3	2	1
7.	My overall rating of this book is	5	4	3	2	1

Comments:

Project Self-Reflection

Topic _____

Name _____ Date _____

As I think about the research project I have just completed, I am especially pleased about

_____

_____

I think this turned out so well because _____

_____

The most important thing I learned while working on this project was _____

_____

If I were to improve one thing about my project, I would _____

_____

My next goals is _____

_____

Research Presentation

Oral Presentation of Research

Name _____ Date _____

Topic _____

	Working on it		**OK**		**Great**

My Research

1. I used resources.	1	2	3	4	5
2. I took notes and organized ideas.	1	2	3	4	5
3. I prepared visuals for my audience.	1	2	3	4	5

My Presentation

1. I spoke clearly so everyone could hear.	1	2	3	4	5
2. I maintained eye contact with the audience.	1	2	3	4	5
3. I made it interesting to the audience.	1	2	3	4	5
4. I presented it in an order that made sense.	1	2	3	4	5

I was best at _____

_____

I would like to improve _____

_____

_____

Writing Self-Assessment: Intermediate

Writer_____

Topic _____ Date _____

The Organization of My Writing

☐ Information is organized around topics.

☐ There are headings to help the reader.

☐ There is an interesting beginning.

☐ The end summarizes key ideas.

☐ There are topic sentences.

☐ A reader could identify a key word or phrase for each paragraph.

Visual Supports

I provided the following visuals to support my information

_____

☐ The page(s) are organized so that visuals and text appear in interesting configurations.

☐ There is a table of contents, index, glossary, captions, and/or

_____

☐ I have shared my writing with others to check the clarity of the content.

☐ I have edited my work.

☐ While writing this piece, I learned _____ about the craft of writing informational texts. (Use additional pages if necessary to reflect on what you learned.)

Interactive Assessment

Have your students select an example of informational learning to celebrate. The chosen item can be a project, a piece of art, a piece of writing, and so forth. The student then is responsible to write on the form on page 225: "I am proud of this because." The teacher adds a positive celebration in the middle section and then the work goes home for the parent to add a positive comment in the last section. The comment sheet and the work come back to school and can be shared through private conferences with the teacher, through group sharing sessions, or considered as a portfolio addition.

It can be especially meaningful if this is done monthly so the parents get used to focusing on positive points in student work samples.

Monthly examples can also be kept together so parents can reflect each month on progress made since the beginning of the year.

Example

Ways of Football

A swift kick will transport the football down the field
to start the first half
A split second pass could save you from a sack
to the wide receiver
A single catch will get you a touchdown
producing six points
A smart hand off could give you a first down
leading to a new set of downs
A successful team will do all of that
and triumph over their opponent.

By: Trenton

Example

PARENT PAGE
Interactive Assessment Form

Date ___5-27___

Student

I am proud of this because ___I usually not ~~verry~~ very good at writing poetry and this proves I pretty good at poetry.___

Teacher

I am proud of this because ___Trenton showed his willingness to use the mini lesson to extend a poem he already started.___

Parent

I am proud of this because ___I feel that Trenton is good at writing if he would just let it flow, and this shows that.___

Interactive Assessment involves students, teachers, and parents in shared celebration of progress!

These interactive assessment samples were provided by Glenda Haley, of St. Joseph, MO.

Example

Forever

If everything and everyone lived forever
Would we run out of things to do?
Would the world be tired of living
Would the world become friends
with the stars
Would frogs begin to talk?

If everything and everyone lived forever
Could we paint the world
a different color?
Would we learn to have 18 jobs,
ride a bike, swim,
and fly in an airplane all at once.
Would we invent something
to see the golden gates of heaven?
Like a mirror, mirror on the wall

If everything and everyone lived forever
Would the sun take vacations
every once an a while
Would we have cures
for cancer in our suitcases
Would doctors
lose their jobs
Would we even have
cancer any more?
If everything and everyone lived forever
Would snow stop falling?
Would forever be too long?
Written By: Emmaleigh

Example

PARENT PAGE
Interactive Assessment Form

Date _____5-26_____

Student

I am proud of this because _I didn't really think that I had poetry in me. When I wrote this I guess I was just starting to think about the future ahead of me._

Teacher

I am proud of this because _Emmy really let her personality shine through. She told the whole story, not just a few lines_

Parent

I am proud of this because _Emmy did a lot of deep thinking and questioning! She took a step as a writer and worked hard as a poet to use a variety of stages poets use — strong words, emotions, mental images, etc. line breaks, etc._

These interactive assessment samples were provided by Glenda Haley, of St. Joseph, MO.

Interactive Assessment Form

Date _____

Student

I am proud of this because _____

_____

_____

_____

Teacher

I am proud of this because _____

_____

_____

_____

Parent

I am proud of this because _____

_____

_____

_____

Afflerbach, P., P.D. Pearson, and S.G. Paris. 2008. Clarifying Differences Between Reading Skills and Reading Strategies. *Reading Teacher* 61(5):364–73.

Allington, R.L., and S.A. Walmsley. 2006. *What Really Matters for Struggling Readers: Designing Research-Based Programs*. 2nd ed. Boston: Pearson/Allyn & Bacon.

———. 2007. *No Quick Fix, The RTI Edition: Rethinking Literacy Programs in America's Elementary Schools*. New York: Teachers College Press.

Beers, K., R. Probst, and L. Rief. 2007. *Adolescent Literacy: Turning Promise into Practice*. Portsmouth, NH: Heinemann.

Block, C.C., and M. Pressley. 2002. *Comprehension Instruction: Research-Based Best Practices*. New York: Guilford Press.

Britton, J. 1992. *Language and Learning: The Importance of Speech in Children's Development*. Portsmouth, NH: Boynton/Cook.

Calkins, L. 1993. *The Art of Teaching Reading*. Boston: Pearson.

Calkins, L., M.C. Cruz, M. Martinelli, et al. 2006. *Units of Study for Teaching Writing, Grades 3–5*. Portsmouth, NH: Heinemann.

Calkins, L., and The Teachers College Reading and Writing Project. 2003. *Units of Study for Primary Writing: A Yearlong Curriculum*. Portsmouth, NH: Heinemann.

Cole, A. 2003. *Knee to Knee, Eye to Eye—Circling in on Comprehension*. Portsmouth, NH: Heinemann.

Dorn, L., and C. Soffos. 2005. *Teaching for Deep Comprehension: A Reading Workshop Approach*. Portland, ME: Stenhouse Publishers.

Duke, N.K., and J.M. Moorhead Reynolds. 2005. Learning from Comprehension Research: Critical Understandings to Guide Our Practices. In *Spotlight on Comprehension*, edited by L. Hoyt, 9–21. Portsmouth, NH: Heinemann.

Duke, N.K., and P.D. Pearson. 2002. Effective Practices for Developing Reading Comprehension. In *What Research Has to Say About Reading Instruction*, 3rd ed., edited by A.E. Farstrup and S.J. Samuels, pp. 205–42. Newark, DE: International Reading Association.

Duke, N.K., M. Pressley, and K. Hilden. 2004. Difficulties with Reading Comprehension. In *Handbook of Language and Literacy Development and Disorders*, edited by C.A. Stone, E.R. Silliman, B.J. Ehren, and K. Apel, 501–20. New York: Guilford Press.

Elly, W.B. 1992. How in the World Do Students Read? IEA study of reading literacy. The Hague, Netherlands: International Association for the Evaluation of Educational Achievement.

Fountas, I., and G.S. Pinnell. 2001. *Guiding Readers and Writers, Grades 3–6: Teaching Comprehension, Genre, and Content Literacy*. Portsmouth, NH: Heinemann.

Freeman, Y.S., and D.E. Freeman. 2009. *Academic Language for English Language Learners and Struggling Readers: How to Help Students Succeed Across Content Areas*. Portsmouth, NH: Heinemann.

Harvey, S., and A. Goudvis. 2000. *Strategies That Work*. Portland, ME: Stenhouse Publishers.

———. 2007. *The Comprehension Toolkit: Language and Lessons for Active Literacy*. Portsmouth, NH: Heinemann.

Harwayne, S. 2002. Non-Negotiables in Teaching Reading. Presentation at the Beaverton Literacy Conference, Beaverton, Oregon.

Hilden, K., and M. Pressley. 2007. Self-Regulation Through Transactional Strategies Instruction. *Reading and Writing Quarterly* 23(1): 51–75.

Hoyt, L. . 1992. Many Ways of Knowing: Using Drama, Oral Interactions, and the Visual Arts to Enhance Reading Comprehension. *Reading Teacher* 45(8): 580–84.

———. 2002. *Make It Real: Strategies for Success with Informational Text*. Portsmouth, NH: Heinemann.

BIBLIOGRAPHY

———. 2004. *Exploring Informational Texts: From Theory to Practice*. Portsmouth, NH: Heinemann.

———. 2005. *Spotlight on Comprehension: Building a Literacy of Thoughtfulness*. Portsmouth, NH: Heinemann.

———. 2007. Interactive Read-Alouds series (K–1, 2–3, and 4–5). Portsmouth, NH: Heinemann.

———. 2008. Mastering the Mechanics series (K–1, 2–3, and 4–5). New York: Scholastic.

Jensen, E. 2008. *Enriching the Brain: How to Maximize Every Learner's Potential*. New York: John Wiley and Sons.

Johnston, P. 2004. *Choice Words*. Portland, ME: Stenhouse Publishers.

Keene, E. 2008. *To Understand: New Horizons in Reading Comprehension*. Portsmouth, NH: Heinemann.

Keene, E., and S. Zimmerman. 2007. *Mosaic of Thought*. 2nd ed. Portsmouth, NH: Heinemann.

Miller, D. 2002. *Reading with Meaning*. Portland, ME: Stenhouse Publishers.

Opitz, M.F., and M.P. Ford. 2006. *Books and Beyond: New Ways to Reach Readers*. Portsmouth, NH: Heinemann.

Opitz, M.F., and M.D. Zbaracki. 2004. *Listen Hear! 25 Effective Listening Comprehension Strategies*. Portsmouth, NH: Heinemann.

Pearson, P.D. 2007. Teaching Reading Comprehension: Research, Best Practice, and Good Teaching. Presented at the Florida Reading Association Conference, September 9.

———. 2008. Teaching Reading Comprehension 24/7. Presented at Colorado Council Reading Association, February 7.

Pearson, P.D., and M.C. Gallagher. 1982. The Instruction of Reading Comprehension. *Contemporary Educational Psychology* 8: 317–44.

Pressley, M. 2002. *Reading Instruction That Works*. 2nd ed. New York: Guilford Press.

Purcell-Gates, V., N.K. Duke, and J. Martineau. 2007. Learning to Read and Write Genre-Specific Text: Roles of Authentic Experience and Explicit Teaching. *Reading Research Quarterly* (March).

Resnick, L. 1991. Shared Cognition: Thinking as Social Practice. In *Perspectives on Socially Shared Cognition*, edited by L. Resnick, J. Levine, S. Teasley, 1–20. Washington, DC: American Psychological Association.

Routman, R. 2003. *Reading Essentials*. Portsmouth, NH: Heinemann.

Stead, T., and N.K. Duke. 2005. *Reality Checks: Teaching Reading Comprehension with Nonfiction, K–5*. Portland, ME: Stenhouse Publishers.

Tovani, C. 2000. *I Read It, But I Don't Get It*. Portland, ME: Stenhouse Publishers.

Wilhelm, J. 2002. *Action Strategy for Deepening Comprehension*. New York: Scholastic.

INDEX

INDEX

INDEX

Also Available from Linda Hoyt

Spotlight on Comprehension

Building a Literacy of Thoughtfulness

Edited by **Linda Hoyt**

2004 / 560pp / $37.00

Exploring Informational Texts

From Theory to Practice

Edited by **Linda Hoyt, Margaret Mooney,** and **Brenda Parkes**

2003 / 200pp / $21.50

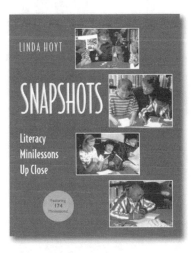

Snapshots

Literacy Minilessons Up Close

Linda Hoyt

2000 / 264pp / $27.50

Make It Real

Strategies for Success with Informational Texts

Linda Hoyt

2002 / 336pp / $29.00

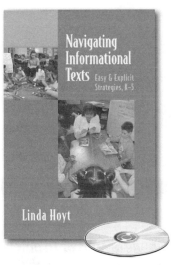

Navigating Informational Texts DVD Set

Easy and Explicit Strategies, K–5

Linda Hoyt

2007 / DVD (approx. 90 minutes) + Staff Developer's Guide / $325.00

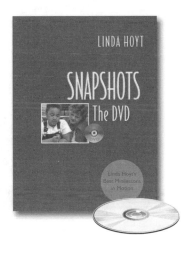

Snapshots The DVD

Linda Hoyt

2007 / DVD (approx. 40 minutes) / $45.00